The Absolute
Beginner's Guide to
BUYING A HOUSE

More Absolute Beginner's Guides

The Absolute Beginner's Guide to Mixing Drinks

The Absolute Beginner's Guide to Taking Great Photos

The Absolute Beginner's Cookbook, Revised 3rd Edition

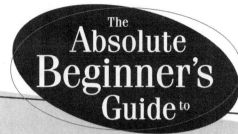

The Absolute Beginner's Guide to

BUYING A HOUSE

Nicholas Ordway

PRIMA PUBLISHING

Published by Prima Publishing, Roseville, California. Member of the Crown Publishing Group, a division of Random House, Inc., New York.

PRIMA PUBLISHING and colophon are trademarks of Random House, Inc., registered with the United States Patent and Trademark Office.

All products and organizations mentioned in this book are the trademarks of their respective companies.

Interior design by Susan Sugnet, Prima Design Team

Library of Congress Cataloging-in-Publication Data

Ordway, Nicholas.
    The absolute beginner's guide to buying a house / Nicholas Ordway.
        p.   cm. — (Absolute beginner's)
    Includes index.
    ISBN 0-7615-3615-9
    1. House buying. I. Title. II. Absolute beginner's guide series.
HD1379 .O73 2002
643'.12—dc21   2002022442

02 03 04 05 HH 10 9 8 7 6 5 4 3 2
Printed in the United States of America

First Edition

Visit us online at www.primapublishing.com

To the firefighters who protect our homes,
to the police officers who protect our safety,
and to our families who protect our souls.

Contents

Acknowledgments

I t takes a lifetime and many friends to gain the knowledge to write a book like this. The team at Prima made it a lot easier. Acquisitions editor, Denise Sternad, served as my coach. Project editor, Libby Larson, was the quarterback. The front line consisted of publicist Matt Jarrette, copyeditors Michael Knight and Ruth Younger, proofreader Linda Ward, compositor Linda Weidemann, and interior designers Susan Sugnet and the Prima Design Team. Backfield coaches were my agent, Grace Freedson, and Jack Friedman, who suggested that I write this book.

Special teams included all of my friends over the years at the Hawaii Real Estate Commission and Hawaii's Department of Commerce and Consumer Affairs, including former commission chairs George A. "Red" Morris, Gloria J. Damron, Marcus Nishikawa, Barbara Dew, and Douglas Sodetani. Also of great assistance and support were Cindy Alm, Robert Alm, former director of DCCA Calvin Kimura, and former Hawaii governor John Waihee.

Mike Sklarz and Harvey Shapiro provided me with coaching and real estate statistics, and Judy Gorman and Bill Chee kept me in touch with national REALTORS organizations and institutes.

Special thanks go to those who chaired the Real Estate Center at the University of Hawaii, including Tan Tek Lum, David L. Ramsour, and Elizabeth Benton. Advisory council members included LaVerne Bessert, Jean Brooks, Aaron M. Chaney, Kenneth Chong, Donald Clegg, Larry Cross, Karen Nakamura, Kent M. Keith, Raymond A. Lesher, John Reilly, Ron Jay Schmid, Edwin Shiroma, Charlene Sohriakoff, Oswald K. Stender, R. Brian Tsujimura, and Gregg T. Yamanaka.

Of particular help were members of my staff at the real estate center, who provided research that serves as background for this book. These include Steve Gilbert, Susumu Ono, Alicia Oh, Rae Gee, Wendy Izumi, Mark Ushijima, Grace Cayapan, and Cynthia Yee. Other individuals at the University of Hawaii who supported this project include Donald Bell, David Bess, Shirley Daniel, Steve Dawson, David McClain, Hamid Pourjalali, Eric Mais, K.K. Seo, Alice Shibata, Marsha Anderson, Nicolaos Synodinos, and Larry Price.

Of prime importance is Kathy Ordway, my main cheerleader.

The Absolute
Beginner's Guide to
BUYING A HOUSE

Finding the Home
of Your Dreams

Isn't it time to buy that dream home you've always wanted? Well, you've just taken the first step. Reading this book will help you find the best home that you can afford. You'll be introduced to strategies that successful real estate agents use to facilitate millions of home purchases. And the secrets you'll learn may even save you thousands of dollars!

Buying a home is, of course, one of the biggest financial commitments you'll ever make, so it's important that you have a plan or strategy to get the most for your dollar. Most people spend from 25 to 40 cents out of every dollar they earn on a home. To put it another way, most people work at least 15,000 to 20,000 hours during their working life to pay for a home and home expenses. Spending a week or two developing a plan or strategy is a small price to pay to get the best home, in the best neighborhood, for the lowest price, and with the most affordable mortgage.

THE EIGHT STEPS TO A SUCCESSFUL STRATEGY

The proven strategy for finding your perfect home is based on the following eight steps, which are described in detail throughout this book.

Step One: Decide Whether You Really Are Ready to Buy a Home

While many people want a home, they are not psychologically prepared for home ownership or do not have their finances in order. Ask yourself the following questions:

Are you really ready to buy a home?
Does everyone in your family see the need to move and find a different place to live?
Will you and your family be better off buying a home or renting?

You will be asked to make a decision at the end of this chapter.

Step Two: Discover Where You Want to Live and in What Type of Home

Chapter 2 discusses how to choose a good neighborhood and what characteristics preserve property values. It also explores the advantages and disadvantages of different housing types, including comparing new houses to previously occupied homes. The chapter gives special attention to problems in buying a new house from a builder and explains how you can find a builder who is reputable. You'll also learn about community associations and special problems with condominium or co-op living. Ultimately, this chapter will

> Most people work at least 15,000 to 20,000 hours during their working life to pay for a home and home expenses.

help you develop a HOME PROFILE summarizing the needs and wants for your dream home.

Step Three: Become Familiar with What's Available in the Market

This chapter introduces you to the role of real estate agents and clarifies whom they represent. If you are not careful, you may find yourself working with an agent who is actually working for the seller and, by law, must forward to his real client all "confidential" information you imprudently share (see the next section, "A Necessity"). You'll learn how you can get full representation, which will not necessarily cost you anything extra. Chapter 2 introduces methods to help you become familiar with housing that's available in the market, including houses available through a real estate broker, houses for sale by owner (FSBOs), and houses that aren't currently for sale but might be if the owners are asked.

Step Four: Pre-Qualify and Get Loan Pre-Approval

Chapter 3 addresses the amount you can afford to pay for a house. This takes into consideration your lifestyle needs as well as your budget. It covers practical suggestions to improve your chances for getting a better and cheaper loan by putting your credit history in order. The chapter also includes a strategy you can use to work with mortgage brokers and other lending professionals. Finally, you'll learn what you must do to pre-qualify for a mortgage loan and receive a written loan pre-approval, including information on the loan application and what the lender is looking for.

Helpful Hint

Using the Internet is a great way to get the information you need to develop your plan and magnify your options. It gives you access to current market information, sources of mortgage financing, and other tools to help make your home search more effective and save you thousands of dollars.

Step Five: Use Professionals, Inspect the Property, and Get Disclosures

Chapter 4 focuses on how to analyze the home and property you are seriously thinking about purchasing. You'll learn what you and your real estate agent need to look for in the house, the site, and the off-site. Before you make an offer, it's usually a good idea to have the property inspected; therefore, the chapter concludes with a discussion of how to select and use home inspectors once you have narrowed your home choices.

Step Six: Negotiate the Deal; Read, and Then Sign the Contract

Chapter 5 discusses negotiation strategies to get the best deal, using different strategies for different markets. The climax of the negotiation is the real estate sales contact. We discuss what should and should not be included in this contract. Because it's usually a good idea to have a qualified attorney advise you on contract issues, the chapter also covers finding a lawyer best qualified to assist you.

> ### Helpful Hint
> Most states today require sellers to provide property condition disclosures that can help in your inspection of the property.

Step Seven: Obtain Your Best Financing

Chapter 6 discusses why you should shop around to find the best mortgage financing available. Topics include how to determine the actual cost of rates and terms and the four factors that create different kinds of financing: the down payment (equity), the interest rate, the term, and the amortization (a big word but a simple idea). The different types of mortgage financing available, including conventional mortgages, FHA, and VA loans, are all covered. We also discuss the advantages of locking in the interest rate as well as the fees and closing costs associated with financing.

Step Eight: Plan Move, Do Walk-Through, and Resolve All Problems

Chapter 7 deals with closing the transaction. This involves the transfer of the deed that makes you the new owner, normally done through escrow. Both escrow and non-escrow closings are discussed. Prior to the closing, you'll need to follow several precautionary steps to avoid being "taken." These include shopping for adequate insurance coverage as well as taking advantage of the final walk-through. The chapter also discusses unresolved problems or last-minute ambushes that can occur before closing.

The last two chapters provide information and help that can be used in several of the above steps. Chapter 9 identifies a wide variety of Internet Web sites that can assist you in your home-buying strategy. Finally, chapter 10 contains answers to frequently asked questions about home buying.

 ## A NECESSITY

In addition to the eight-step plan, a basic but absolutely necessary element of a successful strategy is to identify and use a qualified real estate professional to work for you. Some people will try to take advantage of your lack of knowledge and experience, and this could cost you tens of thousands of dollars that could be saved or spent elsewhere. You should know how to protect yourself from potential crooks, incompetent "professionals," and false friends who would like to take some of your money. Consider the following three examples:

1. Betty and Archie met Molly Broker at an open house. They indicated that they were interested in buying a home. Molly gave them a cup of coffee and asked a number of questions about their finances and how much they were willing to pay for a house. Later that week, Molly showed the couple several houses. They fell in love with a small Cape Code–style home. The

house was listed with Molly's real estate company for $300,000. The couple told Molly that they wanted to make an offer of $250,000 but were willing to go as high as the full $300,000. They also provided other confidential information to Molly, whom they assumed was their "agent." The offer of $250,000 was turned down. Molly urged them to make an offer at the full listing price, which they did. This offer was accepted. Later they discovered that the seller had previously accepted an offer for $225,000, but the deal fell through when the buyer couldn't get a loan. When she was asked to explain, Molly became defensive, telling them that she had a duty to represent her client—the seller. Betty and Archie were "just customers."

> Some people will try to take advantage of your lack of knowledge and experience, and this could cost you tens of thousands of dollars that could be saved or spent elsewhere.

2. Mark and Kim purchased a Spanish Revival–style house that had been built in 1950. They fell in love with the kitchen appliances, the silk drapes in the living room, and the crystal chandelier in the hall. Sasha, their real estate agent, was a friend of Kim's from high school. She had just passed her real estate license exam, and this was her first sale. No home inspector was hired because Sasha said the house was in good condition. She also didn't see the need to stop by the house for a final walk-through because they had just seen it the day before and were in a hurry to close. After closing, they drove to the house and were shocked that the house had been stripped of its appliances, drapes, and chandelier. Later they discovered that the house was infested with termites and the chip-

ping paint contained lead, which could be poisonous to their three-year-old.

3. Jose was promoted to department manager at an Internet company. On the basis of his expected stock options, he borrowed money to buy a car and a time-share in Aspen, Colorado. He went to his bank to pre-qualify for a mortgage loan of $500,000. The loan officer told him that because he had installment debt of $60,000, he could only qualify for a loan of $425,000. Without the loan on the car and time-share, he could have easily pre-qualified for the bigger loan. He was quoted terms of 8% plus two points. Jose failed to shop around. He assumed he could get the best rates from his own bank. However, other banks were offering 7.75% interest without points.

In each of these three cases, real estate professionals served the homebuyers poorly. Betty and Archie discovered that the real estate broker actually represented the seller and was thus duty-bound to forward to the seller all confidential information. As a result, the couple paid too much for the house. Mark and Kim should have employed an experienced broker and not worked with a friend without a track record. It was a blunder not to hire a qualified home inspector and an even bigger blunder not to do a walkthrough the day of the closing. Finally, Jose should have deferred his big-ticket consumer purchases until after he received his mortgage loan. Also, shopping around or working with a qualified mortgage broker would have helped him find the best financing.

 ## AVOIDING COMMON MISTAKES

Your well-executed plan will help reduce the possibility of "buyer's remorse" (when you experience anxiety after a major purchase and think you made a mistake). Let's look at what a homebuyer, especially a first-time buyer, should do to avoid making mistakes and ending up with "buyer's remorse."

Understand the home-buying process. You also need to know the players who can help or hurt you in this process. By knowing the process and the players, you'll be able to anticipate surprises and know who can help you solve problems.

Know your rights as a consumer. This knowledge includes federal and state fair housing laws, equal credit opportunity laws, fair credit reporting laws, and other consumer protection rights.

Research and compare before making an offer. You must understand the market so you know what is available at each price range. Unbelievably, some people spend less time comparison-shopping for a house than they do shopping for a pair of shoes or a home-entertainment system. As a result, they often find that if they had looked around, they could have bought a better house, in a better neighborhood, and at a better price.

Find and properly use qualified professionals. First, you must find qualified professionals who will be loyal to you and not to the seller or have self-serving conflicts (such as a home inspector who also makes repairs). Second, you must know what questions to ask about the different aspects of the purchase process so that these professionals can help you make better decisions.

> Unbelievably, some people spend less time comparison-shopping for a house than they do shopping for a pair of shoes or a home-entertainment system.

Don't Be Afraid of Buying Instead of Renting

Individuals who choose to buy a home often find that they are paying less each month after five or so years than if they had kept paying rents. Don't get trapped into waiting for prices or interest rates to fall. Usually costs go up, becoming just another reason for delaying a purchase decision.

Don't be afraid to buy a home. More specifically, don't be afraid of borrowing the several hundred thousand dollars necessary to buy a middle-class home in today's market. Some people who cannot make this type of commitment will continue to pay higher and higher rents to a landlord without anything to show for it except rent receipts.

Get members of your household committed to the decision. Your spouse, your children (especially teenagers), and other household members can make the house buying and moving process easier or harder. If they are involved earlier in the decision making, the process will be much easier and acceptable. Gaining consensus can reduce family stress and make the experience more enjoyable.

Know exactly what kind of home you need. You should have a pretty good idea of which features you must have and which ones you would like to have. Also consider what kind of house you will need in the near future. You should consider tradeoffs between the features for your lifestyle and a price range that fits your budget.

Know your tradeoffs when you commit to a house. When you qualify for a loan, the lender tells you the maximum amount of money you can borrow. However, if you borrow all that money, you and your family may have to cut out vacations, defer buying a new car, or send your kids to a less expensive private school or college. These personal tradeoffs may not be worth it.

Consider your housing needs in the near future. In order to make buying a house financially attractive as an investment, you ordinarily have to hold the house for at least two to three years to cover the transaction costs necessary to sell your home and buy a new one. So if you are planning to move in the next couple of years, whether because of career changes or for other reasons, you might be wise to consider postponing a house-purchase decision. If you plan to have children or anticipate your elderly parents moving in with you, consider buying a slightly larger home or a home that can be expanded.

Don't pay too much for a home. People pay too much for three main reasons. First, they don't become familiar with the market and prices of similar homes sold. Second, they don't make a low offer to maximize negotiation power. Third, they become emotionally obsessed with a particular home and let this emotion guide pricing decisions. A good real estate sales agent can prepare a Competitive Market Analysis (CMA) for you (see chapter 5). A CMA will tell you the prices at which similar homes in the neighborhood have sold so that you have a better idea of the maximum price you should pay.

Don't let anyone pressure you. A sharp salesperson can pressure you into the wrong buying decision. Amateur

Make Money When You Buy?

You generally make your money when you buy a house and not when you sell it. This may seem strange, but it is true. Your strongest bargaining power is when you are buying, not selling. The money you save when you buy becomes profit when you sell.

buyers (and almost all new buyers are amateurs) can become emotionally involved with a house and become afraid of losing it. An aggressive seller's agent knows this and can pressure buyers into buying a house without examining better alternatives. A superior home may be just around the corner. Submitting to these high-pressure sales tactics may also prevent you from properly inspecting the house and getting enough information about it to make a wise decision.

Buy the bacon, not the sizzle. Think about how hard the house will be to resell. Will other people be willing to pay for those features you and your spouse love so much? Some people buy a house because of its interior decorations and landscaping. This is often true of homebuyers who purchase on the basis of a model home they toured. The actual house they receive, however, may have no landscaping and no interior decorations. Without the decorations, they may be surprised that the house layout doesn't fit their needs and the cost of decorating their shell home will cost tens of thousands of dollars that they do not have.

Use your experienced real estate agent to negotiate.
Real estate agents who represent the best interests of a

buyer can contribute greatly to creating a better deal. The agent may have better insight into effective negotiation strategies. Not all sellers react the same way, and a good agent may know what hot buttons to push that will get the results you want.

Think about an exit strategy. Most people will not live in their first house for their entire lives. In fact, it is common, especially for young people, to move within five years. As such, considering how difficult the house will be to resell is wise. Be particularly wary of houses that have already been on the market for a long period of time (more than four months). If it took a while to sell to you, how long will it take you to resell it?

Maintain or improve your credit rating before applying for a loan. You can take many steps to improve your credit rating. For example, do not change banks, apply for too many credit cards, or buy a big-ticket item like a car on installment debt for at least six months before applying for a mortgage loan.

Pre-qualify and get pre-approved for a loan. Pre-qualifying allows you to know how much money you can borrow. Even better, being pre-approved means that you can negotiate just like a cash buyer. This gives you a lot of bargaining power and can lead to a lower price and other concessions from the seller.

Don't pay too much for a mortgage. There is a wide range of costs and mortgage products available on the market. It is essential that you shop around, usually with the assistance of a mortgage broker, so you can identify the best possible financing package to meet your specific needs. You shouldn't just look at the lowest interest rate without considering total finance costs.

Get the right type of mortgage. There is a wide range of different mortgage loan products. Depending on your earning pattern and plans for the future, some products may be better than others.

Get a written rate lock and good-faith estimate. Without a written commitment as to the interest rate and finance charges, you may be very surprised that interest rates, points, and other finance costs can jump up when the time comes to close the deal.

> **Helpful Hint**
>
> Price is not the only consideration in a good deal. Some concession from the seller may be worth more than just a reduction in the price. Issues such as who pays the closing costs and other expenses could reduce the amount of down payment required at closing.

Choose a good location. When purchasing real estate, location is one of your most important concerns. A good neighborhood located near your place of work, good schools, recreation facilities, religious and cultural resources, and places to shop can significantly improve your quality of life. Check out the different neighborhoods in a community and find the one that fits your family's needs best.

Check out neighbors or community associations. Incompatible neighbors can lead to some of our most stressful problems. For example, a person allergic to cats would have a real problem with a neighbor who has twenty cats to keep herself from being lonely. In condominiums and community home associations, homeowners are sometimes subject to the whims of elected officers and boards of directors. These elected neighbors are sometimes worse than landlords at interfering with your life and privacy.

Investigate legal restrictions on your home. Many communities have deed restrictions that may prevent you from changing the color of your house, adding fences, storing boats or other recreational vehicles, or even keeping certain kinds of pets. In addition, zoning, subdivision regulations, and building and housing codes may put additional restrictions on what you can do with your home. In some cases, if your house doesn't conform to the legal restrictions, a judge may order you to correct the problem. This could result in having to make expensive modifications or your house being torn down.

Get legal help. Surprisingly, some people never read the contracts and other documents they receive. They take the word of real estate agents or lenders that these are "standard forms" that everybody uses. You should seek the assistance of a qualified real estate attorney to examine all legal documents. In most real estate transactions, the law requires that all promises be written. Generally, oral promises are not enforceable. An attorney can help you make sure that the contract includes all promises made by the seller and others and that the contract is enforceable. In addition to advising you generally as to your rights and obligations, the attorney can help on specific issues such as how you should take title to the property.

> A good neighborhood located near your place of work, good schools, recreation facilities, religious and cultural resources, and places to shop can significantly improve your quality of life.

Buy adequate insurance. It's important to purchase an owner's title insurance policy as well as suitable fire and hazard insurance. Although you may think you can save money by not getting adequate insurance, you may pay the price later should something unforeseen happen.

Stay away from problem houses. Problem houses can be old or new. Problems can include structural defects, inferior floor plans, or simply inadequate size for your family. Termites, dry rot, faulty septic tank systems, and other issues that require serious evaluation may be present. Even worse, some houses suffer from toxic problems such as lead paint, radon poisoning, or electromagnetic contamination. These can have negative impacts on the development of healthy children. Avoid them by hiring a licensed home inspector or engineer to evaluate a home you're considering purchasing before you do so. If you're buying a new house, interviewing others who purchased their houses from the same builder can help you determine the builder's reputation.

Have the land surveyed. Although this step may be unnecessary if your house is within a modern residential subdivision, it can help you reduce your risk if you're purchasing an older house or property with water frontage. You might discover "party wall encroachments" or boundary erosion by water action. Cases in which the house was built on the wrong lot have even been reported! Surveys will also reveal possible easements that may not be in the public records.

Estimate your expenses. One area that often surprises a new homeowner is how much it actually costs to live in and maintain a house. This is particularly true of older houses in which various items such as the roof or the electrical system are wearing out and require expensive repairs. Another consideration is the property taxes. In some jurisdictions, when a house is resold, it is reassessed for property tax purposes. It is not uncommon for property taxes to suddenly double or triple.

Do a final walk-through inspection the day of the closing. This is particularly important if the seller has promised to make certain repairs. If you agree to take title to the house before these repairs are made or fail to set money aside in an escrow account to cover the cost of the repairs, you may be out of luck. These repairs may never be made because of a doctrine called "merger," which is described in chapter 7.

Get a home warranty. Many homebuilders provide home warranties. If the home is found to have defects (usually within two years of the purchase), either the homebuilder will make repairs or the warranty company will pay for another contractor to repair defects. If a new homebuilder cannot provide a home warranty, this is a red flag. Often this means the builder had too many problems in the past. Home warranties are sometimes available for used houses.

Anticipate problems affecting your move. New homebuyers sometimes have unexpected problems when they move from their current home to their new one. For example, if you have a lease with a fixed term, you may have to pay off the landlord if the unit cannot be rented to a new tenant at the same rent you were paying. If you know you will be looking for a house soon, sign a month-to-month lease if possible. Another issue is allowing the seller to hold over as a tenant after title has been transferred. This is almost always a bad idea. Exactly how are you going to remove the tenant-seller when you want to move in if he or she wants to stay?

Now that we have covered some of the factors that will help make your home-buying experience a success, let's review the disadvantages and advantages of buying a home.

THE DISADVANTAGES OF BUYING A HOME

Sometimes, a decision to buy or not buy may depend on your personal situation. If your personal situation is likely to change in the near future, you may be wise to wait until things stabilize to buy your home. For example, are you planning to move because of possible job changes or a promotion, are you planning to get married or divorced, are you planning to have a child, or are you planning to retire?

When deciding whether you should buy a home, you need to weigh the disadvantages with the advantages. These are grouped into the following financial and lifestyle considerations.

Financial Considerations

- *Initial high costs and reduction of personal cash savings.* Buying a home involves an initial financial commitment necessary for the down payment. It also requires you to pony up monthly mortgage payments, which usually include a pro rata share of property taxes and insurance. The down payment may sharply deplete your savings. The monthly payments may reduce the disposable income you could have used for other purposes.

- *Added costs for maintenance and repairs.* When you rented an apartment, the landlord paid for most of the maintenance and repair costs. As a homeowner, you will pay plumbers to repair leaks, electricians to rewire obsolete electrical systems, and other service providers to make various repairs. Alternatively, you can spend your time making the repairs yourself if you know how.

- *Taking on a large debt burden.* Houses are not cheap. Few people have sufficient money saved up to pay cash for a home. To borrow money, you have to commit yourself to paying back a large sum over a very long time. This long-term commitment scares many people.

- *Need for more furniture and other household items.* Most people spend an estimated 10% of the house price to decorate it and buy indoor and outdoor furniture. Typically, you are increasing your space when you purchase a home, and human nature is to fill that space with additional possessions.

- *Less money available initially for entertainment or other discretionary spending.* At first, you are likely to pay more each month to own a home than to rent one. The good news is that most of your expenses are relatively stable. So while your former landlord is raising the monthly rent each year, you are now paying off your loan with mortgage payments that usually don't change (unless you have an adjustable-rate mortgage, or ARM, which we'll talk about in chapter 6).

- *Lack of money for investments in other assets such as stocks or bonds.* Because paying off your mortgage creates in essence a forced savings program (you're accumulating equity in your home), you usually have less money to invest in the stock market. This means that you'll have less to talk about with your hairdresser or barber when the stock market collapses or booms. This is not to trivialize the upside potential of stock investing; however, the slower and less exciting returns from real estate investments have generally outperformed most stock and bond portfolios. Slowly increasing your total assets while your house appreciates in value and you pay off your loan may seem boring to you.

> Most people spend an estimated 10% of the house price to decorate it and buy indoor and outdoor furniture.

- *Hard to sell house quickly if you need to move or need money fast (illiquidity).* It typically takes at least three months to sell a house in most markets, thus your home is less "liquid" than most assets. In some markets, selling may take a couple of years—unless the seller is willing to discount the price sharply.

- *House values can fall.* While houses in most markets appreciate (increase in value) at or above the rate of inflation, this is not always the case. Real estate markets tend to be cyclical (prices go up and down). Sometimes, prices can actually decrease. For example, if you live in a town with a single large employer and that company closes the plant, this situation is likely to have a negative impact on house prices.

  > Selling a house is usually more time-consuming than buying one.

- *Possible foreclosure.* If you lose your job, get sick, get a divorce, or suffer other tragedies, you may not be able to make your monthly mortgage payments. This could result in the bank foreclosing on your home, which means you will be renting again.

Lifestyle Considerations

- *Reduced mobility.* Because reselling your house is both time-consuming and expensive, owning a home reduces your ability to move spontaneously. Moving will require planning that you cannot do quickly. Selling a house is usually more time-consuming than buying one. You may find that hard to believe, but it is true.

- *Time must be devoted to maintaining the property.* You must spend more time mowing the lawn, maintaining the landscape, cleaning fallen leaves from the gutter, shoveling the snow, repairing broken windows, and doing other chores. Or you can pay others to perform these tasks (and perhaps find yourself spending as much time waiting for these people to show up!).

- *Possible lack of group amenities.* In many apartment complexes, you may have a swimming pool and clubhouse, tennis courts, and other group amenities. Although you can also have these in a condominium home, unless you are relatively well-to-do, you're unlikely to have all these amenities with a single-family home.

- *Possible longer commute time to job.* Most people buy homes in the suburbs, which often results in longer commuting times to their places of work. This is particularly true of east coast cities.

- *Requires more time and involvement in community affairs.* When you buy a home, you will discover that becoming involved in the community is important just to protect your property values and make sure you get fair access to municipal services paid for by your tax dollar. Yes, renters also pay taxes, but these are part of the monthly rental payments charged by the landlord. When you pay property taxes directly, this somehow inspires you to become more interested in how these taxes are spent.

 ## THE ADVANTAGES OF BUYING A HOME

Everyone needs someplace to live. You can own or you can rent. What some people perceive as advantages may seem burdens to others. To help assess your priorities, consider the following.

Financial Considerations

- *Credit improvement.* Homeowners who have made prompt mortgage payments generally have a better credit rating than do renters, which makes borrowing money in the future easier, particularly if you plan to move up to a better home.

- *Stability in long-term housing costs.* Renters see their monthly payments go up year after year. Homeowners, especially those who have standard fixed-rate mortgages, see little change in their monthly housing payments. The good news is that after several years, the monthly housing payments will generally be lower than the rental market. The best news of all is that after the mortgage is paid off, the homeowner will own the house free and clear.

- *Investment.* Buying a home means investing in a relatively safe asset. Home values are likely to go up. Because most buyers have borrowed money to purchase their home, the earning potential from appreciation is magnified.

- *Possibility of future equity refinancing.* When property values increase and the mortgage loan is paid down, the homeowner's equity grows. It is then possible to get a home equity loan. Unlike interest paid on credit card balances, the interest on home equity loans is tax deductible.

- *Tax advantages.* Mortgage interests and property taxes are mostly deductible. When you sell a primary residence, the capital gain for up to $500,000 (for a couple in the year 2002) is not taxable. Since the Tax Relief Act of 1997, it is not necessary to reinvest in another primary residence. You might also qualify for home office deductions as well as other attractive tax-reduction possibilities. Because of the tax breaks, most homebuyers can afford to pay about 30% more each month in mortgage payments compared to monthly rent.

Lifestyle Considerations

- *Prestige and pride of ownership.* Home ownership often leads to a feeling of pride, as is reflected in well-maintained and landscaped homes. Homeowners often take pride in their flower gardens as well as interior decor.

- *Strengthens a sense of community responsibility and involvement.* Homeowners typically have a vested interest in improving their community and becoming involved in neighborhood affairs. Their high voting rates, attendance at public meetings, and membership in community organizations are evidence of their concern.

- *Control and space.* Homeowners usually enjoy more interior and outside space, which families with children and large pets find particularly useful. Because they can modify their premises without written permission from a landlord, homeowners are kings and queens of their own castles.

- *Access to better schools.* Homeowners usually have access to better schools for their children. Most local public schools are funded by local property taxes. Taxpayers are often effective in demanding accountability from school administrators for improving the quality of teaching.

- *Positive psychological impact on children.* Studies at Johns Hopkins indicate that children from owned homes do better in school, both academically and socially, than do children from rented homes.

- *Possibility of improved personal safety and security.* People often move into the suburbs, and gated communities, to improve their safety. Although apartments can mimic some of a home's safety features, in most minds apartment living is just not the same as living in a home that you own. As a result of terrorist attacks on America, some people are less comfortable in high-rise rental properties in urban areas.

 ## DECIDING WHETHER YOU REALLY ARE READY TO BUY A HOME

The decision is yours. Weigh the advantages and disadvantages. Then decide what is best for you.

If you have decided that you are ready to buy a home, you have taken the first step. Congratulations!

Finding a Place
Before You Find a Home

An obvious step after you've decided that you need or want to buy a home is to select a real estate sales agent. But wait! You need to do some homework so that a sales agent can't stampede you into buying something you don't want, a decision you could regret for years to come.

Before you focus on a specific house, decide where and in which kind of neighborhood you wish to live and what features and type of house you want in your dream home. *Beware:* If you don't do your *own* homework, you could be disappointed. Consider the following example:

> Peter and Wendy, who lived out of town, chose Mr. Hook as their agent. He took them to a beautiful neighborhood, where he drove them past a large park with wonderful trees and landscaping. They found a home on a crystal blue stream, just two houses away from the park. Mr. Hook realized that Peter and Wendy had fallen in love with this house and pressured them to make a quick decision. On the first night they moved into their dream house, they awoke to a horrible smell—a cross between

A Strategy to Avoid Buying Problem Houses

It cannot be emphasized enough that any home you buy should be carefully inspected several times—by you, your agent, and a qualified, licensed professional home inspector. Figure 2.1 illustrates the three major steps in performing an inspection:

Figure 2.1

FIND, COMPARE, SELECT, INSPECT, AND INSPECT AGAIN

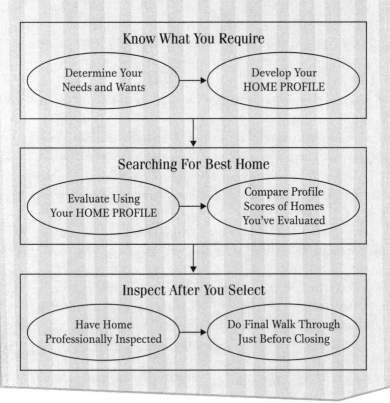

bubble gum and cow manure. They soon learned there was a huge sewer treatment plant right next to their neighborhood and that the plant tried to mask the odor with a perfume-like chemical. On week-

Location, Location, Location

Homeowners often realize after their purchase that the choice of neighborhood may be even more important than their choice of house. You can always modify a flawed house, but all you can do about a bad neighborhood is move out.

ends, the park turned into a teenage hangout and area drug distribution center. When it rained, the stream turned brown and flooded their basement.

 ## SO WHERE DO YOU WANT TO LIVE?

Even before you approach a sales agent to represent you, you need to know something about the neighborhoods in your community.

Neighborhoods are areas within a city that contain homes of a similar type. They often have cultural, ethnic, and/or other population characteristics as well. For example, some neighborhoods are characterized by families with children, others by "swingles" (swinging singles) or retired persons. Families with children are often attracted to neighborhoods with good schools, churches, organized sports for children, and other facilities focusing on families. Some neighborhoods are built around golf courses, tennis centers, or other recreational facilities that attract those who enjoy these activities. There are even neighborhoods in the United States that attract pilots who can park their private planes at the community airfield bordering their backyards. By looking around, you can find neighborhoods that best suit your personal tastes, recreational needs, and other desires.

Searching for the Perfect Neighborhood

To start your search, get a detailed city map. AAA is a good source. Another source for maps is the city or county planning departments, though they may charge a fee. Maps can identify neighborhoods, zoning restrictions, future land use, and transportation plans. The U.S. Department of Agriculture sells topography maps as well as maps on soil distributions.

Helpful Hint

If you belong to AAA, you can get street maps for free.

Using a map as a base, start by marking locations that you and your family visit often or that are important to you. For example, consider where you and your spouse work; where family and friends live; the location of doctor's offices and hospitals, schools, child care facilities, parks; and other key features. Select neighborhoods that are convenient to all or many of these places. Use a highlighter or crayon to connect all the places you marked. Then start looking for potential neighborhoods where most of these lines cross.

You can get information about the nature of these neighborhoods from your sales agent. However, even a well-informed sales agent will not be able to help you actually choose a neighborhood. Both federal and state housing laws prohibit real estate agents from the discriminatory practices of "steering" and "blockbusting." Steering is when a real estate agent shows only houses in neighborhoods occupied by people similar to you on the basis of race or similar criteria. On the other hand, blockbusting occurs when sales agents try to inject racial fear into neighborhoods so property owners panic and sell at low prices. For these reasons, sales agents have to be careful when providing information on neighborhoods. Some sales agents will not share information about crime rates, quality of schools, population characteristics, and similar data.

Check out public information you obtain from the city and county as well as on the Internet. Both are good sources of information.

See for Yourself

Once you have identified and collected some background information on possible neighborhoods, it's important to check them out for yourself. Don't take anybody's word for the quality of a neighborhood. For over thirty years of teaching real estate, I have always advised, "You have to get out there and kick the dirt."

To start with, take a drive or walk around each neighborhood to get a feel for its personality—*without* your sales agent. Agents selectively drive in the nice areas of the neighborhoods and avoid the eyesores. While walking around, talk to some of the residents.

> ## Helpful Hint
>
> You can research neighborhoods via online sites that contain pertinent information on schools, crime rates, and such. Be sure to try the following sites:
>
> homeadvisor.msn.com
> homestore.com
> realtor.com
>
> On most such sites, you can bring up area information by entering a zip code or address. These sites are also great for looking up market information about recent home sales and availability of listed homes.

Ask what they like or don't like about living there. You'll find them surprisingly frank and informative, revealing details that you cannot easily observe or find in public records or Internet databases.

While visiting neighborhoods, you should consider a number of factors including the following:

Location

Location is one of your most important decisions when buying a home. It involves the physical location of the property as well as access both to and from the rest of the community.

The "journey to work" (simply put, the time it takes to commute to work) is a key decision-making factor. Most people don't want to spend more than about forty minutes commuting each way. While checking out neighborhoods, try driving from your prospective home site to work—and back—during rush hour. Consider the distance to highway networks, park-and-ride lots, and public transportation, as well as the traffic jams—keeping in mind that they will be worse when it rains or snows. Pay attention to the direction of the sun on your commute to work. Facing the sun on your drive to work and again on the way home is no fun. Try different routes to see whether any shortcuts can reduce your travel time.

> The time it takes to commute to work is a key decision-making factor. Most people don't want to spend more than about forty minutes commuting each way.

Where do the families of both you and your spouse live? Do you want them to be near or far? The answer may depend on factors such as how much you need free babysitting services or desire your privacy. Where do your friends live? Keep in mind, however, that if your friends are young, they will likely move in the near future, just as you are planning to do now.

Pollution and Noise

Be sure to consider the distance from the neighborhood to sources of pollution or noise. Certain kinds of pollution can affect your health and quality of life. Don't choose a spot downwind from cow pastures or sewer treatment plants, for example. Although sales agents often say you get used to odors, they still affect you. Also find out whether the neighborhood is affected by or effectively buffered from noise coming from nearby expressways, railroad tracks, airports, industrial activity, nearby schools or child care centers, and other facilities.

Reputation and Prestige

For some, the prestige of a neighborhood is important. Most of us have heard of Beverly Hills, Gross Pointe, Highland Park, Buckhead, Kahala, Boca Raton, Manhattan's Upper East Side, Georgetown, and other prestigious neighborhoods that dot the country. Homes in such districts command a price premium of hundreds of thousands of dollars. While most of us must settle for less, we would still like to live in comparatively upscale neighborhoods. If you are new to the city and interested in prestige, find out which neighborhoods are considered elite. In addition to the status you gain as a resident, neighborhoods that top the hierarchy also better maintain home values.

Community Pride

A neighborhood with a greater percentage of homeowners usually preserves its value and quality better than one with a higher percentage of renters. Walk around a neighborhood and see how the houses and yards are maintained. Are streets and sidewalks littered? Is house paint peeling? Have leaves been removed from the gutters, or do little bushes grow in the gutters? A neighborhood that isn't maintained is a neighborhood in decline. Avoid such areas. Likewise, a neighborhood in which houses are being remodeled and older houses

> A neighborhood with a greater percentage of homeowners usually preserves its value and quality better than one with a higher percentage of renters.

torn down and replaced by nicer houses indicates a revival in progress that will likely lead to appreciation in property values. Buying during a revival can be a good investment because prices may be low initially, but once the neighborhood is fixed up, prices often rise quickly.

Child Safety Information

Numerous Web sites, most based by state, are dedicated to child safety. A good nationwide site, www.stopsexoffenders.com, contains lots of information on how to keep your children safe from harm.

Megan's Law requires that sex offenders be registered and the community notified about where they live. Some crime statistics and information on sex offenders can be found on the Internet (some sites are listed in chapter 9).

Safety

Safety is extremely important to most homebuyers. Signs that people feel safe in their neighborhoods include children playing in the yards and parks without visible adult supervision as well as clean, well-maintained landscaping throughout the neighborhood. On the other hand, iron bars on doors and windows, graffiti and signs of gang territories, and abandoned cars exhibit an unsafe neighborhood. Almost every city contains areas with signs of decay. The farther or more buffered your neighborhood is from blight, the safer you might feel. Keep in mind, however, that burglars and other criminals like to go where the money is, and that's often to neighborhoods that appear safe. So check with the local police about local crime statistics. Because of safety concerns, homes are often sold with security systems. Also, gated and other planned communities with private security personnel in the suburbs and guarded condos and co-ops in the cities are increasingly popular.

The Look and Feel of the Neighborhood

Physical characteristics can add to or subtract from a neighborhood's attractiveness. Large lot sizes and building setbacks can open up the neighborhood and make it appear less crowded. Street designs that feature an internal system of curved roads and cul-de-sacs create one image; grid patterns form another. Many suburbanites appreciate amenities such as golf courses, parks, playgrounds, jogging or bicycle paths, and ponds and streams. Others prefer a dense, packed environment with local grocery stores, shops, restaurants, and nightclubs—all within a town setting. What appeals to you and others in your household depends on your lifestyle and preferences.

Schools

Many experts believe that school quality is the most important factor affecting property value. Even if you have no children and do not plan to have any, buying a home in an excellent school district pays off in the long run, when you resell your house. Check with the local school district and ask for national test scores, student-teacher ratio, and average spending per student. Also ask parents whose children attend school in the neighborhood for their opinion.

Amenities

Easy access to shopping and restaurants is often important. In the suburbs, you can expect to drive to the grocery store if you need a gallon of milk; however, you want the drive to be short, not halfway across town. In

> Even if you have no children and do not plan to have any, buying a home in an excellent school district pays off in the long run, when you resell your house.

the city, where residents often depend on public transportation or walking, nearby grocery and drugs stores are even more important. Certain people, particularly elderly citizens, may wish to be near medical facilities. Others, such as disabled citizens, may need specialized public transportation. In addition, some individuals look for nearby public recreational facilities—tennis courts, golf courses, running or bike paths, health clubs, and so forth.

Utilities

You may consider utilities to be about the same everywhere, but they're not. In fact, just crossing a street might put you in a different power or telephone district. So it's a good idea to find out what companies supply the utilities to the neighborhood and to ask residents during your walk-throughs what the average rates are and how service is. In addition to electricity, gas, and telephone, see about cable or broadband access as well as water, garbage collection, and sewer. Some neighborhoods are not linked to public sewer systems, so the homes require functional septic tank systems. Utilities can be a huge hidden cost of moving, especially if you are currently a renter not used to paying these bills or now live where services are less expensive than in the neighborhoods you are considering.

Restrictions

If you find a house that isn't quite perfect, you may decide that, with a little work, it can be. You may want to change the exterior paint color, add an extra room, or keep a horse. Even though the house will be yours, limitations in the local zoning ordinance or the subdivision's conditions, covenants, and restrictions (CC&Rs) might keep your house less than perfect. Check for any restrictions you can't change before locking yourself into a house. Tell your agent what, specifically, you plan to do with the house and ask her to find out whether it's allowed.

Taxes and Special Assessments

If you're renting, property and other related taxes are included in your rent. As a homeowner, however, you will be responsible for paying these taxes in addition to your mortgage. Although you can find out what taxes the previous owner paid, some tax districts automatically reassess any

Why Is It For Sale?

While you drive through a neighborhood, notice whether the neighborhood has few or many "For Sale" signs. Lots of them can mean that the neighborhood is very "hot" and homeowners are hoping for a great profit by selling. On the other hand, it may be a sign that homeowners are bailing out. One neighborhood I visited had many "For Sale" signs on one side of the road and none on the other. A little research revealed a power transmission line near the backyards of the homes for sale that had an impact on the residents.

home that's sold. Therefore, the tax you will pay may be very different from the tax the previous owner paid. Ask your sales agent to check this out. While investigating each neighborhood, pay attention to whether the roads have potholes, the sidewalks have significant cracks, or public workers are laying new pipe or building expensive facilities in the neighborhood park. The local government or district may impose a special assessment on each property owner in the neighborhood to pay for planned repairs or improvements. This might mean that you'll receive a bill for thousands of dollars if you buy a home in that neighborhood.

Sales Statistics and Trends

Talk to your real estate agent. He or she can get you sales statistics for the neighborhoods you are considering. These often show price trends, time on market for new listings, and other valuable information. Most multiple listing services allow agents to run statistical analyses. However, some agents don't know how to access and use this information. If your sales agent cannot or will not share this information, consider getting one who will. You want an agent whom you can trust as well as one who knows how to do the job correctly.

The Condition of the Neighborhood

As you are visiting each neighborhood, consider the current condition of the neighborhood as well as how it may change in the future. Planners and economists know a neighborhood typically goes through a life cycle that lasts fifty to seventy years. The phases of the cycle include growth (increasing property values), stability (stable property values with increases for inflation), decline (falling property values), and possible revitalization (called "gentrification," with significantly increasing property values). How can you judge the condition of the neighborhood and determine which cycle it's in? Well-maintained houses and yards suggest stability. Broken windows, peeling paint, and overgrown lawns suggest decline. In-fill development, rehabilitation of old houses, and rental tenants being replaced by homeowners are all signs of gentrification.

Community Associations

While you're considering neighborhoods, as well as condominiums, co-operatives, and townhouses, checking out the community associations (CAs) that govern them is important. Today, approximately 60% of new houses purchased in urban areas are part of community associations. In the United States, there are approximately 150,000 CAs with roughly 40 million members. These associations are particularly common in planned subdivisions, planned unit developments, and planned new towns.

Community associations are called different things depending on where they are located. "Homeowners' association," "property owners association," "common

> Approximately 60% of new houses purchased in urban areas are part of community associations.

interest community," "common interest development," "common interest realty association," and "residential community association" are common terms for CAs. They are created by a "declaration" or a "master deed," which your real estate agent can find in the public records.

Community associations are important because they control what you can and can't do to the exterior of your house, within your yard, and in the common areas of the neighborhood or the condominium. Control is exercised through enforcement of "conditions, covenants and restrictions" (CC&Rs) in your deed. CAs may impose mandatory monthly fees for operations and maintenance or make periodic special assessments for capital improvements such as a new tennis court. Monthly fees can amount to hundreds of dollars. Both fees and assessments can usually be increased or issued without a membership vote. If you fail to pay these, the association can bring a foreclosure lawsuit against you in court. Some areas include a second association within the first that imposes an additional set of fees to operate a golf club or tennis center. Membership in the second association may be voluntary, but membership in the first is usually mandatory.

> Community associations control what you can and can't do to the exterior of your house, within your yard, and in the common areas of the neighborhood or the condominium.

Investigating the community association is extremely important when considering areas in which to live. Most CAs are well run and greatly enhance the neighborhood or condominium; however, my personal research indicates that as many as 20% are dysfunctional. Officers and directors can become power-mad and dictatorial in enforcing CC&Rs, especially those who get themselves elected to boards for the sole purpose of getting even with a neighbor they don't like. Such people can be more intrusive than landlords or even the government. Disputes and even lawsuits sometimes arise that turn neighbor against neighbor over trivial matters. One dispute in my hometown resulted in over $100,000 in legal fees to resolve a matter costing only $750 to fix. Such disputes can poison relationships forever and make a community a miserable place in which to live.

If you decide to buy a home in a CA, you may be restricted in what you can do with the house. Most CA regulations cover exterior paint colors and treatment, height of walls or fences, outdoor lights, sheds, basketball hoops and playground equipment, existence of home businesses, noise, landscaping, length of grass, and so forth. Some don't allow you to store equipment outside or dictate the types of pets you can own. Others have been known to prohibit storing baby carriages and bicycles on the front lawn, outdoor barbecues, hanging Christmas lights, Halloween decorations, or displaying the American flag except on the Fourth of July! If you want to do something not allowed in the CC&R, you often have to ask to be put on the agenda for a board meeting and then appear in a public hearing to get permission from your neighbors.

Problems in a CA can lead to a decline in property values. Unusually low current prices in a CA as compared to similar neighborhoods is a red flag that something may be wrong. While a low price may be a genuine bargain, it's important to look into the CA for a potential problem you won't want to deal with later.

When looking at a neighborhood that has a CA, you should do the following:

1. Talk to potential neighbors and ask them whether they are satisfied with the association. Also ask about any problems between the association and any neighbors.

2. Ask your sales agent to investigate the reputation of the CA and how it operates.

3. Ask the CA manager or an officer whether the association is or has been involved in any lawsuits. If the association budget has a line item indicating high legal fees, this is a sign that the CA may be or has been in litigation.

4. Ask to see the financial statements and operating budget of the association. Also look at the bylaws, management agreements, and rules.

5. Talk to one or more of the officers or members of the board of directors.

6. Check the monthly maintenance fees and ask whether any special assessments are anticipated.

7. Read the CC&Rs and have your real estate attorney examine them to make sure that you can make any changes to the house or store equipment such as an RV or boat outside the house.

8. Ask your attorney to explain any restrictions in the declaration or a master deed.

> If you are a free spirit who likes living your own life without being told what you can and cannot do with your property, a CA is probably not for you.

While community associations can be good for a neighborhood, make sure you can afford the fees in your monthly budget and are prepared for those fees to rise at any time. Also, you must be willing to submit to additional rules and regulations that could change on the whim of the board of directors. If you are a free spirit who likes living your own life without being told what you can and cannot do with your property, a CA is probably not for you.

What Type of House Do You Want?

A wide range of housing types—from new single-family, detached houses to condominium units—can be found in most housing markets. Because each type has its own strengths and weaknesses, you will need to make tradeoffs that can impact your planned lifestyle. To make the best choice for your family, take time to weigh the pluses and minuses of each home type. Let's look at your choices.

A New Single-Family House

For most people, a new home is their ideal choice. The fact that you are the first owner makes new homes appealing. Everything in the house is new: the roof, the appliances, and the heating and air-conditioning system. New houses, on average, tend to be bigger and have more bathrooms than older homes. If the house has not been built yet or is currently under construction, you can often make some customizations, such as choosing kitchen appliances, wallpaper, or floor treatment or adding a Jacuzzi or game room. Building codes have improved during the past few years, resulting in improved energy efficiency because of double-paned windows and better insulation. The electrical wiring is capable of carrying the power requirements of modern appliances and computers. Many houses are "smart," meaning they are cable-ready and have broadband access. If you are one of the first buyers in a new subdivision, you can often get a better price and more amenities or upgrades than if you are among the last ones to buy. By the time the subdivision is complete, prices will have risen and, within that time, your property value will have appreciated.

Almost all builders provide warranties on their homes. These typically cover almost all defects for the first year and then provide reduced warranty coverage for subsequent years. Better programs, called 2/10 warranties, provide very

A Previously Owned House

Some people prefer to buy a previously owned home. Usually you get more for your money. Also, many older houses have superior craftsmanship as well as better quality wood and masonry work. Most new homes today are built using wood from second-growth forests. This wood is less dense than wood from old-growth forests.

Unlike dealing with builders of new homes, you have a better opportunity to negotiate the price for a used home with its seller. You may even get the seller to practically give away appliances, curtains, and furniture. Because the neighborhoods of used homes are already established, you can see the condition of the landscaping. You can also meet your neighbors in advance. Many "new house" problems have already been solved, and the house has completed most of its settling process. In other words, what you see is what you get. You are not looking at a model of what your home will be like; you are looking at the actual home you will buy.

Problems with a Used Home   While used homes have some advantages over new homes, they also have their own unique problems. Previously owned houses may have wiring or plumbing that needs to upgraded. There may not be enough electrical outlets, phone jacks, or cable connections. The roof may need to be replaced. Bedrooms tend to be smaller and bathrooms fewer, perhaps inadequate for your family. Older houses (those built prior to 1978) may contain

> Older houses (those built prior to 1978) may contain lead paint and asbestos, both of which are dangerous, especially to children.

lead paint and asbestos, both of which are dangerous, especially to children. Older houses are usually less energy efficient. Insulation, if any, may be old and need replacing.

Buyer Beware: Foreclosures

Foreclosures often look like great deals, especially those that are only a year or two old. However, former owners who have lost their homes due to a foreclosure often leave destruction. They have been known to tear out the wiring, pour cement into the pipes, break bathroom fixtures, and smash walls and windows. Once they are through, tearing down the building and starting over may be less expensive than trying to fix all the damage.

Also, an older home may not have central air-conditioning and heating. As a result, you may end up spending much more on gas and electricity to heat and cool a small old house than you would a larger new house.

Watch out for "fixer-uppers" or "handyman's specials" and foreclosures. These houses can be real money pits, forcing you to spend more money purchasing and fixing up the house than you would buying a new home. Although they are sold for prices that appear to be below the market, you may run into problems that are exceedingly expensive to correct. Fixer-uppers are usually houses that have come to the end of their economic lives, so stay away.

If you are interested in purchasing a used home, here are suggestions to protect yourself:

1. Negotiate, negotiate, and negotiate.

2. Inspect, inspect, and inspect. While you should always inspect a new home, it is even more important to inspect a used one. Hire a professional inspector who knows what to look for. You'll find this more than worth the cost.

3. Have the sellers provide you with a written disclosure of property condition. This is required in some states. If they sell the house "as is," which means you are accepting the house with all its problems and defects, have them disclose the specific defects that you are taking "as is."

4. Have an attorney draft a contract to include all agreements, including which fixtures and personal property are included. Everything must be in writing. If the seller said he would leave something, make sure it's in the contract.

5. If you decide to buy a fixer-upper, get a loan that includes money for renovation, such as an FHA 203(k). It is usually cheaper than getting a home improvement loan, and the interest may be tax-deductible. Besides, you should consider the repairs and renovations part of the price of buying this type of home.

6. If you are buying a foreclosure property, check out special loan programs. Use an agent who is an expert in foreclosure sales. These agents are worth their weight in gold and can save you money and headaches when you move in.

7. Did I mention negotiate and inspect?

Manufactured and Mobile Homes

Manufactured or factory homes (which include mobile homes) are quite popular; they account for one of every four new homes built in the United States. About 18 million people live in this type of housing. These homes are built in a factory, then shipped to the site in pieces, assembled, then installed on a permanent foundation. Although some manufactured homes are of the same high quality as homes built on site, others are disasters waiting to happen.

A major advantage of manufactured homes is their cost. They cost an average of approximately half as much per square foot as a house built on site. Therefore, you'll get more space for your money. Also, in 1974, the U.S. Department of Housing and Urban Development began to regulate quality standards (Manufactured Home Construction and Safety Standards). Each manufactured house has to have on the rear of the house a data plate (a "red tag") with a serial number. This tag certifies zones for which the house was constructed, including wind resistance, thermal qualities, and roof-load capacity. These factors are particularly important if you live in areas with high winds, snow, or extreme temperatures.

> A major advantage of manufactured homes is their cost. They cost an average of approximately half as much per square foot as a house built on site.

Although manufactured homes are less expensive to purchase, they generally make a poor investment. They lose value much like cars do. Rarely, if ever, do they go up in value. In addition, lenders provide financing through retail installment contracts, which are more expensive than regular home mortgage loans.

Manufactured homes also generate a high level of complaints. Surveys show that over half of the manufactured houses have at least one major problem. One study by the AARP found that nearly three-quarters of members surveyed had major problems with defects and only about one-third of these problems were resolved under warranties. In fact, inadequate warranties are a common complaint of owners. This is not surprising because most warranties do not cover defects caused while the house was being transported to the site or defects due to improper installation. Improper installation accounts for about half of all problems reported by consumers! To make matters worse, only a few states require that installation be covered by warranties.

Most owners lease land in manufactured home parks. Once located in a park, you are at the mercy of the park landlord because moving a manufactured home can cost thousands of dollars. Once these homes are installed, they are usually there permanently, unless blown away by a hurricane or a tornado. Surveys show that over half of the owners of manufactured homes had sharp increases in land rent or increases in the costs of services such as water and garbage removal. Landlords usually reserve the right to approve new purchasers or renters. By rejecting qualified potential purchasers, landlords may force you to sell the house to them at a sharp discount. Cost of legal services to combat this unfair practice can be more than an old home might be worth in the first place. Besides, wasn't one of the main reasons for purchasing a home to get away from landlords and increasing rent?

If you plan to buy a manufactured home, take the following precautions:

1. Buy your own lot or move into a resident-owned park.

2. If you decide to rent space for your manufactured home in a park, interview the existing residents to find out how the landlord treats homeowners who rent space. But remember, landlords can change.

3. Check the reputation of the home manufacturer. Check with your state consumer protection agency or the attorney general's office and the Better Business Bureau.

4. Talk to owners who purchased homes from this manufacturer and ask about any problems and how warranty claims were treated.

5. Read the warranty carefully and try to get coverage for problems occurring during transportation and installation.

6. Hire a home inspector or professional engineer to supervise the installation. After the home is installed, have it inspected carefully for any defects that may be covered by the warranty.

7. If you are buying a previously owned manufactured home (about 20% buy from the previous owner), have it carefully inspected.

8. Contact a HUD-approved housing counseling agency for advice. HUD's Housing Counseling Clearing House can be called at 1-800-569-4287 for an automated referral to a local agency.

Condominiums

Evaluation of condominiums (condos) is similar to evaluating new or previously owned homes. However, it's important to understand the legal differences between a condo and a house. When you own a condo, you will have an interest that is owned in common with other people. Your life, and your investment, can be impacted by what they do (see the previous discussion on community associations).

A condominium is a special type of ownership. You are buying two different things: First, you buy an individual unit that you own personally. Second, you buy a share in common elements owned as a group by the people in your development. Common elements may include hallways and elevators in a high-rise building, swimming pools, tennis courts, roofs, parking lots, and other features shared by everyone in the project. It is extremely important to have your attorney examine the following documents: the public offering statement, the condominium declaration (or master deed), the condominium plan, the bylaws, the operating budget, the management deed, and the unit deed.

Find out whether your individual unit begins where the exterior walls begin or where the wallpaper begins. In other words, do you own the walls or just the space between them? Find out what the rules are. Talk to existing owners to see whether they have any problems. Be sure to inquire about monthly maintenance fees and whether the project has enough money in reserve for major repairs, like replacing the roof (which is usually community property). If not, you may have to pay for a special assessment, especially if the building is old and needs a lot of repairs. Determine whether your unit also includes one or more designated parking spaces and storage facilities.

It's a very good idea to get copies of minutes for the board of directors' meetings for the last two or three years. These will show past problems as well as future assessments that may be upcoming. Look to see whether the same problems are addressed over and over again and how quickly problems are resolved. These documents alone can give you insight on how the condos are run.

Townhouses   A townhouse is like a condominium except that you own the land under your unit. If you don't personally own the land, you are in a condominium.

Cooperatives   A cooperative (co-op) is similar to a condominium except you don't actually own real property. Instead, you own stock in a corporation that owns the real estate. This stock includes a proprietary lease that entitles you to occupy a particular unit. In other words, you own a part of an apartment building and get to live in one of the units. You can be evicted if you violate the co-op rules. In addition, co-ops often retain the right to approve new purchasers. This is important because if another tenant fails to make his monthly payments, you and the other tenants will have to make up the difference. If the corporation fails to make or is late on its mortgage payments, the building could be foreclosed and you could lose your property. Except in New York or Chicago, it is unlikely that you'll be involved in this form of ownership.

DEVELOPING A HOME PROFILE

Now that we have discussed the importance of location as well as the various types of homes available, it's time for you to design a HOME PROFILE. This will help you pick the right home in one of the neighborhoods you've already looked at and decided would be fine for your family and lifestyle.

Think of a HOME PROFILE as a report card for evaluating prospective homes. It provides a systematic way to evaluate each home rationally and then compare them. Every family will have their own unique HOME PROFILE, which weighs various criteria by its importance to your family. Your dream house should get a perfect score on the profile. Then, by rating homes, you can see which comes closest to your dream.

A HOME PROFILE is essentially a list of those features you want in a home, divided into categories, with a maximum score provided for each item. Categories need not be worth the same number of points. For example, a maximum score for square footage may be twenty points while included amenities such as a fireplace and ceiling fans may be worth only five points. Categories that are more important to you should be given a higher number of maximum points. Figure 2.2 provides a sample HOME PROFILE.

When putting together your HOME PROFILE, you must consider the future as well as any special needs or desires you may have. For a moment, put the house out of your mind and concentrate on your lifestyle. What do you like to do? What are your responsibilities? What will your family be like in five, ten, or twenty years? If you don't have children

Figure 2.2 **HOME PROFILE**

Needs	Wants	Comments	Bonus Points
3 bedrooms	Extra bedroom	Expects more children in 5 years	5 for extra room
2 full baths	½ to 1 full extra bath	Two baths can get crowded with family of 4	5 for ½; 10 for full
	Walk-in closet in master bedroom	Want access to all clothes, keeping some in storage	3
Kitchen with eating area	Formal dining room	Entertain only occasionally, but would like Thanksgiving and Christmas dinners	5
Family room	Formal living room		5
House size: at least 2,000 square feet	More space	More space would be nice	1 for each extra 100 square feet
Attic storage space	Finished attic	Could use finished attic as guest bedroom	10
Basement storage space	Finished basement	Could use basement as a workshop, but prepared to finish myself	5
Laundry			
Carport	2-car garage		5 for 2-car garage; 8 for 3-car garage
Lot at least 30,000 square feet	More land	Family enjoys outdoor activities	1 for each additional 2,000 square feet
	Dishwasher		2
	Disposal		1

(continues)

Figure 2.2   **HOME PROFILE** (*continued*)

Needs	Wants	Comments	Bonus Points
	Fireplace		2
	Modern electrical wiring	May want to use more appliances and computers; don't need but REALLY want	10
	Backyard deck	Outdoor entertaining, but can build	3
Relatively new house			10 if less than 3 years; 5 if less than 5 years; 3 if 10 years or less; minus 1 for each year older than 10 years
	Swimming pool	Love in summer, but hassle in winter.	2
Location in neighborhood			Excellent = 5 Good = 3
View			Excellent = 5 Good = 3
	Security system	We can always put one in	2
Neighborhood choice		We have identified 5 neighborhoods we like	Neighborhoods A&B: 15 Neighborhood C: 10 Neighborhood D: 5 Other: 0

now, do you plan for some in the future? How about pets—do you own a dog, or do you want a horse? What are your hobbies? In which sports or recreation do you like to participate? Once you've considered your lifestyle, fit the pieces together to determine the requirements for your dream home.

Depending on the size of your family, calculate the number of bedrooms and bathrooms you will need. If a member of your family is disabled or requires special access, be sure this is included. Also consider whether you may have to take care of an elderly relative. Next figure out other types of rooms you will need. Do you want a home gym, a workshop, an office, or a playroom? If you are a gourmet cook, you might need a gourmet kitchen. Maybe a big living room is a must for your large-screen TV and home theater. Because you are dreaming up the perfect house, don't limit yourself during this phase. The sky's the limit.

Don't forget the yards, both front and back. Do you want a lot of space between you and the street? Do you want a pool or a tennis court—or both? How about space for a garden or even a stable?

Next begin to list the various amenities you want in your dream home. These can include fireplaces, patios, bathroom fixtures, and so forth. How about a sink in the garage or an indoor laundry room? Do you require an attached garage? Space for how many cars?

Once you have listed all features you want, divide them into categories and give each one a certain number of points. Make copies of your HOME PROFILE and take them with you as you look at different homes. While going through homes, mark down which items that you want are present and then rate the home by the various categories. Total up the number of points to see how close the home comes to your dream house.

If you have determined where you want to live, in what type of home, and what you want in a home, you have taken the second step. Congratulations!

WHAT'S AVAILABLE IN THE HOUSING MARKET?

As you drive around looking at various neighborhoods, you will become more familiar with the market. In addition, you should investigate a wide variety of information sources— newspaper advertisements, real estate magazines (which you can get for free from your grocery store), and real estate shows on both television and radio. You can even use the Internet to access market information. Take notes and create a special file on your computer to organize information.

A highly effective way to learn about the local market is to visit open houses and tour model homes. Sometimes neighborhoods, especially in historic districts, have a showcase of homes to raise money for charities. Take some time to visit shops near the neighborhoods that interest you and talk to the storekeepers who are owner/operators. Beauticians and barbers can be particularly informative. Also consider visiting the local churches, temples, or other places of worship. Priests, ministers, and rabbis are usually quite knowledgeable about their local areas.

If you have determined what is available in the housing market, you have taken the third step. Congratulations!

3

Minding Your C's

When lenders consider you for a loan, they look at your capacity, credit, character, and collateral. To do this, they use tools such as your credit application, your credit report, and your credit score. If lenders like what they see, you'll usually get better terms in your loan. Therefore, understanding how your credit is established is extremely important. Sometimes the most innocent actions can destroy your credit rating. Consider the following example:

> Romeo and Juliet were recently married. They moved into a mobile home with a loan from Fly-by-Night Finance Company. The couple also applied for a dozen new credit cards in their joint names and cancelled their older cards. Because some of their new cards offered frequent flier points, they charged these cards up to the maximum credit limit. They just kept the other cards in their wallets. When the couple decided they wanted to buy a new home, they applied to many different lenders on the Internet. They also filed applications with a builder and a couple of local mortgage brokers. On the applications, they indicated that they could borrow any needed money for a down payment from their

grandparents. Romeo and Juliet were surprised when they were turned down because of a low credit score. They had no idea why this happened, especially because they had qualified for so many credit cards.

Except for getting married, Romeo and Juliet did almost everything wrong. In this chapter, you'll learn how *not* to make the same mistakes they did. Here we discuss the credit and the loan underwriting process. (For information on how to choose a loan and the various types of loans available, please see chapter 6.)

 ## PRE-APPROVAL EQUALS POWER

It's important to get pre-approved for a mortgage loan before you negotiate for a house. When you're pre-approved, you know exactly how much money you can borrow. This allows you to focus on a specific price range of homes. In addition, your negotiating power is strengthened. The seller realizes you're a serious buyer with confirmed cash and that the deal can be closed quickly.

There is a difference between being pre-approved and pre-qualified. Pre-qualification only lets you know how much you can borrow *if* your credit is okay. Even if you are pre-qualified, the lender makes no commitment to loan you any money. Instead, you're essentially provided an estimate of your borrowing power. On the other hand, with a pre-approval, you have a real commitment. The only additional verification the lender needs in order to give you the money is an appraisal and a title search once you've selected your house.

 ## THE MORTGAGE MARKET

To better understand the process of getting a mortgage loan, you need some background on how the mortgage market works. This market has two main parts: the primary market and the secondary market.

- *The primary market* is composed of lending institutions that make loans directly to consumers like you. If an institution keeps the loans that it makes, it's often called a "portfolio" lender. These lenders are primarily credit unions, savings and loans, and banks. Portfolio lenders can be more flexible and offer more creative loans than lenders who turn around and sell the loans they originate to the secondary market.

- *The secondary market* consists of institutions like Fannie Mae, Freddie Mac, and others that buy loans from primary lenders and mortgage bankers. They then package these loans into mortgage-backed securities, which are similar to bonds, and sell them on the world capital markets. Before a loan can be sold, it must be a "conforming" loan. This means that both the borrower and collateral must meet certain credit standards. A loan that fails to meet these standards, a "non-conforming loan," is kept in the loan originator's portfolio and cannot be sold unless it can be classified as "seasoned." This occurs once the borrower has made timely monthly payments for a set period of time. Because over 60% of all loans are sold into the secondary market, some lenders have very

> ## Helpful Hint
>
> Many different sites on the Internet provide mortgage calculators. Two good ones are:
>
> quicken.com
> www.homepath.com (Fannie Mae)
>
> At the Quicken site, go to the home loans section. At the Fannie Mae site, choose Calculators, then select the True Cost Calculator. Both sites are quite good and will even help you find lenders. For more information on these sites, please see chapter 9.

strict underwriting standards that must be met by the borrower so the loan will conform. You'll find a description of these standards later in this chapter.

UNDERSTANDING THE MORTGAGE LOAN PROCESS

Figure 3.1 illustrates the loan process. Mortgage transactions are complicated and can be very time-consuming and frustrating. Predatory lenders often take advantage of poorly informed borrowers and intimidate them with paperwork, math, and mysterious words and phrases. Don't get cheated. Become familiar with the mortgage process, learn what's available in the money market, and find yourself a good advisor to help you through the process.

First, prepare a budget to see how much you're spending each month and for what. One of the main reasons people can't get good mortgage loans is because they don't save enough money to make the down payment and to pay closing costs. Although a larger down payment can result in a smaller and less costly loan, for most, accumulating a reasonable amount will take several years. You can't borrow money for a down payment from a bank. Some equity lenders do provide money for partial down payments called "second mortgages." Lenders will also need to know how you obtained the money, especially if you didn't have it a couple of months ago. The money can be a present from a relative; however, the lender will want to see a "gift letter" in which the relative agrees that the money does not have to be paid back. In addition, the rela-

> One of the main reasons people can't get good mortgage loans is because they don't save enough money to make the down payment and to pay closing costs.

Figure 3.1
MAJOR ACTIONS IN MORTGAGE LOAN PROCESS

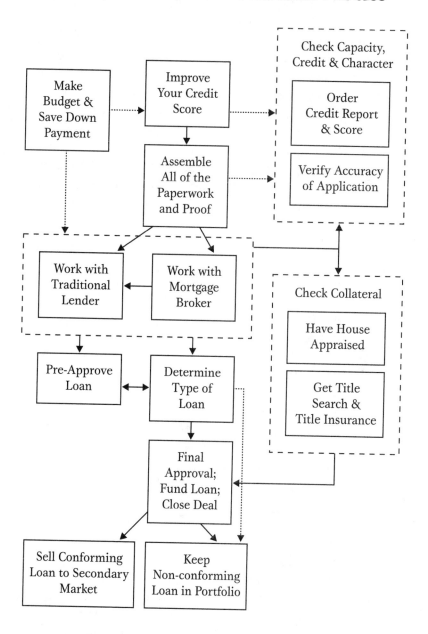

tive may have to produce financial records to prove the source of the gift.

The most important factors influencing the lender's decision are your credit history and what's called your "FICO" score. (FICO stands for the company that tabulates these scores. This company is Fair, Isaacs & Company.) Much of this chapter covers how you can improve your FICO score. When you submit your application, the lender will ask you to include several different documents showing your income as well as your financial responsibilities. Find out what the lender needs early in the process so you can put it all together in advance rather than hold up your application while you search for these documents. Missing even just one item could delay the loan process. Following is an example of some of the documents you must include with your application:

- The sales contract for the house
- Federal and state income tax returns (two years)
- W-2s (two years)
- Most recent paycheck stubs from all employers
- Cancelled checks of child support or alimony payments
- Bank statements (the last three months)
- Statements for IRAs
- Rental agreement
- Gift letter and proof of giver's resources
- Documentation of court-ordered payments
- Certificate of Eligibility (VA loans)

 ## LET'S GO LOAN SHOPPING

Though you may not realize it now, you'll end up paying more for the loan than you will for the house. How can this be? If you buy a house for $250,000, put down $50,000, and get a loan for only $200,000, how can paying back the loan cost more than the house? Not including closing costs (discussed in chapter 7) with a 30-year loan at 8% interest, you end up paying $328,336 just in interest over the life of the loan. That's a lot of money, so shouldn't you invest some time in finding a way to get the best loan for the best price?

Most people call a few lenders with good rates listed in newspaper ads or rely on the lender recommended by the builder or their sales agent. Those are also the reasons most people pay too much. Loans that sound good over the phone may have hidden costs you don't learn about until after you have paid your application fees and the cost of your credit check. It's easy for a telephone salesperson to make a loan sound too good to be true. If it sounds too good to be true, . . . well, you know the rest. As for financing through the seller, in chapter 5 you'll read why that is also often not a good idea.

Most builders suggest a lender. Although this can be convenient, the lender may be owned by the builder and you'll end up paying more than if you find a loan on your own. However, in some cases, builders arrange for special financing with a reduced rate and buy-downs, which may be the best deal in town, but you have to be familiar with what's available in the market to know whether it is indeed the best deal.

Using your sales agent to find a lender can also be risky. For example, your sales agent may try to steer you to a lender that is a captive of the agent's real estate company, and you may again end up paying too much. On the other hand, your sales agent may direct you to a loan officer who can be extremely helpful because he is familiar with the agent and the needs of her clients. Some sales agents know lenders who may have exactly the right loan program for you. They can also direct you to special programs for new homebuyers that are funded by local revenue bonds.

Your best bet is to comparison shop. If your sales agent and lending experts realize that you understand what's available in the market and at what prices, they are more likely to offer you the best terms. Don't forget to check the Internet for Web sites that can bring you up to speed on the current mortgage market in your local area. You'll find some listed previously in this chapter as well as in chapter 9.

It's important to find someone you trust and who is willing to work to get you the best loan. Finding a reliable person is more important than finding a specific lending institution. Decide whether you will use a loan officer at a specific institution or a mortgage broker who can shop around to find you the most appropriate loan.

Either way, you should begin by talking to your friends who have recently borrowed money. If they have had good experiences, ask them if they would recommend the person who worked with them. Also look at newspaper ads, television commercials, and the Internet and create a list of possible lenders. Make appointments for interviews with these lenders and be prepared to ask and answer questions. If the loan expert is evasive, vague, dismissive, or doesn't seem to give satisfactory answers to your questions, find someone else. Remember, you need someone you can trust and who will be upfront with you. You need to decide whether to use a loan officer or a mortgage broker. Let's take a look at the differences between the two to see which would serve you better.

> If your sales agent and lending experts realize that you understand what's available in the market and at what prices, they are more likely to offer you the best terms.

Loan Officers

Loan officers work for a single lender, most often a bank. They can only offer you loans provided by their bank so will not shop around for you. It is best to check out your personal bank. If your family has used the bank for a number of years, you or another family member may even know the officer personally. In those cases, the officer may aggressively represent your case to the loan approval committee. Banks often make non-conforming portfolio loans that allow you to qualify for a loan even if your credit is weak or the collateral is risky. If you have business dealings with the bank as well, it may even make available to you as a preferred customer special loans and other services. You may also be able to set up a direct electronic payment program. Often, this can give you a cheaper interest rate and save you money.

Mortgage Brokers

Mortgage brokers are not tied to a single institution thus can shop around for the best loan. Because they do this for a living, they can usually find a better loan than you would on your own. Some brokers regularly deal with thirty of forty different lenders. They are also very good at finding special programs for first-time buyers. Nearly 70% of all residential home loans are handled by mortgage brokers. They usually make their money through a mark-up or loan origination fee on top of the price quoted by the wholesale lender, typically one point (or 1% of the loan amount), but it could be higher.

> Nearly 70% of all residential home loans are handled by mortgage brokers.

Although mortgage brokers can find good deals for you, they are only indirectly regulated by the federal government, and some states require little or no regulation or licensing. This means that anyone can say he is a mortgage broker and can charge whatever the market will bear or whatever he can persuade borrowers to pay. Let's look at some of the problems you could run into with a mortgage broker:

1. Some brokers steer borrowers away from the best rates or best loans to lenders who pay the brokers a higher fee called "yield spreads." In other words, if the borrower is persuaded to pay a higher rate, the broker will be rewarded with a higher commission. These fees

must be disclosed in what's called the RESPA statement (described in chapter 7).

2. Some brokers do not fully disclose whom they represent. Borrowers may be led to believe brokers are representing them, when in fact they are actually representing a number of lenders.

3. Some brokers are incompetent or lazy and don't return
your calls or answer your questions.

Have the broker list his total fees, as well as who pays them,
in writing. Ask questions and ask for references. If you
aren't satisfied with the answers or services, find someone
else. However, do all of this before you pay any fees or sign
any contracts with the broker.

IMPROVING YOUR C'S

The mortgage loan underwriting process is designed to
show the lender that you are a person who is likely to pay
back the loan. The lender will look at your application to
judge the following:

- Capacity
- Credit
- Character
- Collateral

These factors are sometimes referred to as the "four C's." Some
lenders add two additional C's when evaluating borrowers:

- Capital
- Compensating factors

Note that "compassion" is not among the lender's C's. The
lender judges capacity and credit by ordering a credit re-

port. Character is judged during an interview and during the verification of the loan application (see figure 3.1). Liars do not make good borrowers. Now let's take a closer look at each of the C's individually.

Capacity

Capacity is evidence that you can repay the loan. To determine this, the lender analyzes your monthly income from all sources and considers the stability of these sources. Income includes alimony or child support received, social security, pension fund payments, annuities, rental payments, stock dividends, royalties, and other verifiable sources of income. You will need to document both the sources and the amount of this income.

Generally, the lender wants to see that you have been employed at your current job for at least two years. Job-hopping is frowned upon unless you have changed jobs for a promotion or better pay. Remember, they are looking for stability. A person who can't hold a job may not be able to repay a loan. Lenders give extra consideration to those who have just graduated from college or have recently been honorably discharged from military service. If you are self-employed, getting a loan can be a bit tougher. Lenders will often ask you to produce your last two income tax returns. It's important that you are truthful and consistent on all applications. If you're ever audited, the Internal Revenue Service may look at your loan applications to make sure they match with what you've reported to them. California has a pilot program where some lenders and the IRS share loan application information.

Other areas the lender looks at are your current expenses as well as your future expenses—what they would be after you get the mortgage loan. These include the monthly payments on the proposed mortgage loan. The lender will look at your total monthly debt on installment loans that will take more than ten months to pay off, such as car loans, credit cards, and credit payments for furniture, appliances, and other items. Expenses such as alimony and child care obligations are also considered. Each type of loan program and each lender has different standards. For example, conventional loans often have stricter standards than FHA loans. Likewise, some special loan programs, such as those for first-time buyers, will often have looser standards.

Income and expense information is used to calculate two qualifying ratios. The first is known as the "front ratio." It includes the monthly mortgage payment, property insurance, property taxes, and community association fee. The second is the "back ratio." In addition to the front ratio, it adds the monthly cost of paying off your long-term consumer debt. These figures are then compared to your gross monthly income to calculate the ratios. Table 3.1 illustrates these ratios and also lists the ranges within which you need to fit to qualify for a loan.

For example, consider a person who has an annual income of $60,000. This gives that person a $5,000 gross monthly income. Based on a 28% ratio, this means that $1,400 ($5,000 × .28 = $1,400) would be available for total

Table 3.1

Qualifying Ratios	Factors Considered	Percentage Range
Maximum amount each month you can use to pay mortgage expenses: Total monthly housing expenses divided by income	**Monthly mortgage costs:** Principal, interest, property taxes, insurance (PITI), and other costs such as condominium fees	**Front Ratio: 28% to 33%** 28% (conventional) to 33% (special programs) Note: Higher ratios apply if you make a larger down payment.
Maximum amount each month you can use to pay ALL loan costs: Total monthly housing expenses + total monthly debt divided by income	All consumer debt, alimony, child support, and so on	**Back Ratio: 36% to 41%** 36% (conventional) to 41% (special programs)

monthly housing expenses. Using the 36% ratio for all debt, $1,800 ($5,000 × .36) would be available for monthly housing expenses plus all other debt.

Let's now look at how making a purchase on credit can affect your ratios, assuming you are making $60,000 per year. Suppose you were thinking about borrowing $20,000 for a car that would require payments of $450 per month. You already had $400 in monthly debt payments. Consider the following comparison:

	Before Buying Car	**After Buying Car**
Estimated monthly housing expenses	$1,400	$1,400
Car payments	None	450
Other monthly debt	400	400
Total	$1,800	$2,250
Divided by monthly income ($5,000)	36%	45%

Look what happened to your ratio when you borrowed money for the car! Because you had $400 in monthly debt payments, you were already at the 36% maximum for total debt. Buying the car on an installment loan would prevent you from getting the mortgage loan you needed. In fact (assuming the interest rate on the loan was 8%), buying the car would mean that the amount you could borrow with a 30-year loan would be reduced by over $60,000!

Character

Character is based on your past financial history as well

> ### Helpful Hint
> *Rule of Thumb:* Every dollar of consumer debt you borrow over the maximum amount reduces your mortgage loan by three dollars!

as on the loan officer's judgment call. The financial history shows your past behavior in paying debts. The lender will look at whether you made late payments, your checks bounced, your landlord had to take you to court to pay your

The Trust Factor

If you have some minor flaws in your financial history, often these can be overcome if the loan officer makes a personal judgment that you can be trusted. When I bought my first house, I had been employed just for one academic year as a "temporary instructor" at a university. Sixteen lenders turned me down before the seventeenth decided to give me a chance. It didn't hurt that the loan officer for the final lender had been a student in my real estate finance class during the prior quarter. In many situations, that personal relationship with the loan officer will provide a better judgment of "character."

rent, your car was repossessed, or you are in default on your student loans. Big red flags include bankruptcy and a foreclosure on a previous house.

Credit

Your credit report and credit score are used to assess your creditworthiness. Some lenders deal with the credit rating as part of their assessment of your character. Credit is based on a report from one of the three major credit bureaus, while the FICO score (or similar score) is based on the information in the credit reports. Credit bureaus are referred to as "Consumer Reporting Agencies" or "CRAs."

If you have been turned down for a loan, get a copy of your credit report and check to see whether your report contains errors. Inaccurate information may have been included in your file that was supposed to be in someone else's file—for example, in the file of a person whose name is identical or similar to yours. Also, a creditor might have made a mistake. Should you discover an error, write to inform the creditor that the error must be corrected and all credit bureaus must be informed of the correction.

If the CRA made the mistake, it must delete any disputed and unconfirmed information. Normally this must be resolved within 30 days. Once the CRA makes a correction, you can request that a revised credit report be sent to all credit providers who received the original incorrect report during the previous six months.

On the other hand, if an item is verified as true, you can include a brief explanatory note (100 words or less) to explain what happened. If the information is confirmed, but you disagree, you can submit a "Statement of Dispute." Be aware of the fact that both statements will remain in your file for seven years after they are submitted. For some matters, filing a statement might not be a good idea because your statement will be part of your file longer than the original negative report. Strategywise, you might decide not to include an explanation that involves privacy issues, such as a long-term illness, because anyone who orders the report will see that information. Instead, include the information on your credit application that only the lender will see.

> **Helpful Hint**
>
> Under the Fair Credit Reporting Act, you are entitled to a free credit report if you are unemployed and intend to apply for a job within 60 days, if you are receiving public welfare assistance, if you believe you are a victim of fraud, or if you have been denied credit or insurance.

You can also order your credit report for a small fee or for free (in some states). At the time this chapter was written, the fee was $8.50 in most states. In some states (Colorado, Massachusetts, Maryland, New Jersey, and Vermont), you can receive a report free each year (Georgia will provide two each year). For information on how to get your report and whether it will cost you, use the contact information located below.

Equifax
Equifax Credit Information Services, Inc.
P.O. Box 740241
Atlanta, GA 30374
(800) 685-1111
http://equifax.com
E-mail: customer.care@equifax.com

Experian (formerly TRW)
National Consumer Assistance Center
P.O. Box 2002
Allen, TX 75013
(See Web site for local addresses in the U.S.A.)
(800) 397-3742
(800) 972-0322 (for deaf or hearing-impaired)
http://www.experian.com

TransUnion
P.O. Box 2000
Chester, PA 19022
(800) 888-4213
http://www.tuc.com

Your Credit Score
Your credit score is very, very important. It will determine whether you can get a loan, how much you can borrow, and how much the loan will cost. This section describes what a credit score is and how you can take practical and common-sense steps to improve your score. This is one of the most effective steps you can take toward getting a good loan.

Credit scores, referred to as FICO scores, are based on a secret statistical model developed by Fair, Isaac & Company. Almost every lender relies on these scores. Because they are based on the credit reports of the three major credit bureaus, each borrower will have three separate FICO scores, which range from 300 to the mid-800s. Most scores fall between 600 and 700. The higher the score, the better your access to less expensive credit. Only 2 out of 10,000 loans scoring 800 or higher have become delinquent for at least 90 days.

> Your credit score is very, very important. It will determine whether you can get a loan, how much you can borrow, and how much the loan will cost.

If you score 700 or higher, some lenders will give you a break on the interest rate ranging from ⅛% to ¼%. Usually, a score of 620 means that the borrower is "conforming" and the loan can be resold to the secondary mortgage market. On the other hand, if you score below 550, you may have to find a loan with a "sub-prime" lender. The chances of these borrowers being 90 days delinquent are approximately 5,000 out of 10,000, or one in two. Lenders grade loan applicants on the basis of their FICO scores. A grade of "C" restricts you to the least desirable loans. The following table provides an example of how most lenders grade:

FICO Score	Grade
720 and higher	Excellent (A++)
689–719	Very Good (A+)
620–679	Good (A)
580–619	A–
550–579	B
480–549	C

Your lender determines what credit score is necessary to qualify for different kinds of loans. The lower your score, the less money you can borrow and the higher the interest rate. Each lender may have a different threshold for making a loan decision, which is why it's important that you shop around.

Credit Reports

Get copies of your credit reports at least three months before you apply for a loan and check the reports for accuracy. Request that the credit bureau add any positive information missing from your report and correct any inaccurate information. Normally, the credit bureau must correct unconfirmed negative information within 30 days of being challenged. Removing this information can save you a lot of grief and result in lower interest payments, possibly saving you thousands of dollars over the life of the loan. Studies indicate that from 60% to 70% of all credit reports have errors, with 29% having serious errors that can result in denial of credit!

For a small fee, you can purchase your score from one of the credit bureaus. You'll also receive the top four "reason codes" why your score isn't higher. These reason codes are important because they can show you the best way to improve your score.

Although it's still a secret exactly how your credit scores are derived, you can get a general idea as to what factors make up these scores. Factors that contribute to your score are your financial track record, accounts owed, length of credit history, new credit, and types of credit. Because taking steps to improve your credit score can greatly improve your chances of getting a good loan, here is an explanation of these factors and how you can improve them.

Credit Factor: Track Record (35%) **Explanation:** This is your payment history on credit cards, retail accounts, installment loans, finance company accounts, and mortgages. Serious negative weight is placed on such problems as bankruptcy, judgments, lawsuits, liens, and attachments on wages and chargeoffs. The longer you've been delinquent on your payments, the worse your score. What's important is the number of past-due items and how recent these are. A record of recent on-time payments will improve your score. Many people don't realize that paying rent or utility bills late can have a negative impact on their FICO score. *Warning: FICO considers 30 or more days to be late.*

Improve Your Credit Score: Make sure that you stay current on your bills as early as possible before you apply for a loan—particularly during the three months before you apply. The most current activity counts a lot more than past history. For example, the FICO score considers a 30-day late payment a month ago more serious than a 90-day late payment five years ago. Pay legitimate collection accounts and settle all legitimate chargeoffs with the original creditor. Be sure you get written confirmation that the creditor will have these items removed from your credit report. Closing an account with late payments will not make the late payments go away. Pay early. Don't run the risk of your payment arriving late by waiting until the last possible moment to pay. Also be sure to challenge any late fees assessed to your account if you sent the payment within plenty of time for delivery. Though the fee may seem small compared to the time required to get it removed, you don't want the late payment on your record. Remember, never be late by 30 or more days!

Credit Factor: Accounts Owed (30%)   **Explanation:** Total amount you owe on all of your accounts includes existing mortgages, revolving accounts (credit cards), and installment debts (such as car loans). Although you may not realize it, having a lot of unused credit cards with zero balances hurts your score. It shows the *potential* for a lot of debt. Maximizing your charges beyond 75% of your credit limit on the account is also a negative. On the other hand, if you greatly reduce the amount you owe on the original installment loans, this is a real plus.

Improve Your Credit Scores: Pay down all of your credit card balances below 75% (some suggest below 73%). In other words, if you have a credit limit of $5,000 on your card, make sure the remaining balance is never higher than $3,750 and preferably no higher than $3,650. If you have small amounts on several cards, don't consolidate them under fewer accounts. This increases your percentage of the credit limits that you've used and therefore reduces your FICO score. However, you should cancel unused credit cards and, if feasible, seldom used credit cards unless you have had them for a long time. Also reduce the amount on some of your installment loans, if possible to do so without paying a prepayment penalty.

> ## Helpful Hint
> Don't take on new installment debt before you get your home mortgage loan. For example, hold off on buying a new car, furniture, and appliances, even if you're tempted by a super end-of-year clearance sale.

Credit Factor: Length of Credit History (15%) **Explanation:** How long you've maintained various accounts is an important factor. In other words, longtime loyalty to a credit card company helps.

Improve Your Credit Scores: Keep some of your oldest credit card accounts, even if new cards give lower introductory rates and other sign-up incentives. Be sure to show some activity on these older accounts. Use fewer cards, but use them frequently and make timely payments to improve your credit history. For a long-term strategy, parents should consider setting up their children with a credit card—as long as they use it responsibly. Young people who have proven creditworthy will receive a better FICO score when they apply for their first home loan.

Credit Factor: New Credit (10%) **Explanation:** Opening several credit card accounts shortly before applying for a loan hurts your FICO score. This is especially true for people who don't have long credit histories. In addition, when you seek a new credit card, the company will ask for your credit report. Each time your credit report is accessed, you lose an estimated 8–20 points on the FICO score. *Note:* Requesting a copy of the report for yourself does not affect your FICO score.

Strategies to Improve Credit Scores: For at least twelve months before applying for a home mortgage loan, don't apply for too many new credit cards, even if the company offers bonus frequent flier miles. Newlyweds seeking to buy a house need to be careful, as collecting credit cards may be a natural reaction to their new status. If you plan to rent for the first couple of years, however, this is not as important. Use care when applying with many companies on the Internet for the best home mortgage rates. If these companies access your credit reports, it could have a negative effect. Fair, Isaac & Company tries not to penalize shopping around as long as all credit inquires occur within a few days of each other. Therefore, try to do all your shopping at once rather than over a period of weeks or even months. You want it to appear as though you are shopping for the best rate rather than going from one lender to the next, being turned down, and then reapplying elsewhere.

Credit Factor: Types of Credit (10%)   **Explanation:** Somehow, the mix of your mortgages, installment loans, revolving accounts, and consumer finance accounts is used as a factor in the FICO score. This impact on the score differs depending on each person's credit profile. Some loans, such as those from finance companies, appear to count against you.

Strategies to Improve Credit Scores: If possible, stay away from sub-prime lenders and junior lien financing. These may have an impact on your ability to obtain new mortgage financing.

Now you should understand why our Romeo and Juliet (from the example at the beginning of the chapter) committed financial suicide.

Collateral

Collateral consists of your house and other property that you pledge to secure the loan. If you default on your loan, this collateral can be sold in a foreclosure sale to satisfy some or all of your debt. Because the house you are buying will serve as collateral, the lender requires that the house be worth more than the loan itself. For this reason, the house must be appraised before you are approved for a loan. If the appraisal comes in too low, potential lenders will reject your loan application. The lender also requires a title search and title insurance (see figure 3.1). In addition, each month, typically along with the mortgage payment, the borrower will make additional payments for fire and hazard insurance and property taxes.

Although you pay for the appraisal report, the lender typically orders it from a list of approved appraisers who are licensed or certified to practice in your state. This means that the appraiser works for the lender—not for you. Getting an appraisal on your own is usually not a good idea. The lender may not accept the report and require you to pay for a *second* report.

Normally, the appraiser will base the value opinion on one of three approaches to value—the cost approach, market sales approach, or income approach. Usually, in most active real estate markets, the market sales approach provides the most reliable indication of value. The appraiser selects at least three recent market comparables (sales of similar properties within six months of the appraisal dates), usually from the same neighborhood or condominium project. Adjustments are made for major differences.

The cost approach requires the appraiser to measure the physical dimensions of the property and determine how much it will cost to build a similar or identical structure. A physical inspection is necessary to reveal the condition of the building. Adjustments are then made for physical deterioration and other forms of depreciation. The depreciated cost of the building is added to the value of the land to determine the total value of the property.

In residential appraisals, the income approach is called the "gross rent monthly multiplier approach." Here the appraiser determines the fair rental value and multiplies it times a market-derived factor based on the relationship of rents and recent sales of rental properties. The appraiser normally reports his findings in a standard form called the "Uniform Residential Appraisal Report" (Form 1004).

What If the Appraiser Says the Property Is Worth Less Than You Agreed to Pay?

The first thing you should do is get a copy of the appraisal report. See why the appraised value is less than what you and the seller thought the property was worth. Regulation B of the Equal Credit Opportunity Act requires the lender to notify you of your right to receive a copy of the appraisal. Typically, the lender will send a letter stating that you may make a written request for a copy of the report; however, this occurs only when you have paid for the report. You normally have 90 days to make your request after you have been notified about the lender's loan decision or after you have withdrawn your application.

Once you get a copy of the report, you and your agent should examine it to determine the best strategy. Here are your basic alternatives:

1. Try to convince the appraiser that he or she missed some important information, such as a recent sale that might have been overlooked, or is not yet in the appraiser's databases. If the appraiser is not familiar with a particular neighborhood, you might find a wide variety of information that could change the opinion of property value.

2. Try to convince the lender that the appraiser was wrong and should be overruled or a new appraisal ordered. Let your agent make this argument because, as a professional, he or she is in a better position than are you.

3. Increase your down payment and ask for a lower loan amount. Because the lender is looking for a safety cushion, a higher down payment may satisfy the lender's security needs.

4. Renegotiate the price with the seller. The appraisal is a powerful tool to a fair price reduction. Again, your agent should be the point person in this effort. However, your agent may pressure you to cough up more money to preserve the agent's commission, which is based on the sales price of the house. Take some time to think about this while you're away from the pressure of your agent. You might find a win-win solution that involves both the seller reducing the price and you coming up with some additional down payment.

5. Assuming you included a properly worded financing contingency (following the advice you'll read in chapter 5), you can cancel the sales contract and receive your money back. You will be out the loan application fees; however, if you use the same lender for another home mortgage loan in the near future, you may get a reduction or waiver of some fees for the new application.

6. Appraisers only appraise the *real* property in reaching their opinion of value. This applies to sales contracts that include a great deal of valuable *personal* property (for example, a boat and floating dock on a lakefront property). If this is the case, you may be able to convince the lender to provide additional financing for the personal property and reduce the loan on the real property.

Capital

This refers to how rich you are. Included in this calculation are your savings and other assets like stocks, bonds, and annuities. All of these could be used, if needed, to pay off your loan. In other words, if you can prove to the lender that you don't really need the loan, the lender will fall head over heels trying to lend you the money.

Compensating Factors

Lenders can use compensating factors to make a better loan or even allow a marginal borrower to qualify for an otherwise unavailable loan. These factors ordinarily include something other

> If you can prove to the lender that you don't really need the loan, the lender will fall head over heels trying to lend you the money.

than good credit and steady income, which were already considered in the initial classification of the borrower.

Government programs (FHA and VA) will allow an energy-efficient building to serve as a compensating factor. Income or savings that were not used as qualifying income might also be considered. For example, tax credits for child care or a future pay increase within 60 days of the loan, as verified by a letter from the employer, meet this requirement. Similarly, if your spouse is returning to work in a career for which she or he was previously trained (for example, nurse, lawyer, truck driver), the lender can use your spouse's projected income (confirmed by a letter from the employer) as a compensating factor even if it couldn't be used as a qualifying factor. If you are self-employed and have a large contract that states you will be receiving income in the future, this can also be considered a compensating factor.

Another important compensating factor is if the housing expenses are no more than 10% higher than the rent you have been paying. In other words, if your rent is $1,000 per month, the lender may be willing to let you pay up to $1,100 per month for all mortgage and housing expenses even if this exceeds some of the ratios. Also, if you have at least a three-month savings reserve after paying the down payment and your share of the closing costs, the lender may be persuaded to use this as a compensating factor.

UNIFORM RESIDENTIAL LOAN APPLICATION

For most loans and loan pre-approvals, you will complete the "Uniform Residential Loan Application" (URLA), also called "Form 1003." The URLA is a standard loan application that you complete to begin the lending process. A lender will look at this application, your credit report and FICO score, and other verifying documents to determine whether to loan money to you. Ask your lender to provide you with a copy of this form. Some lenders will help you fill it out, whereas others leave you on your own. This form is also available at many Web sites on the Internet. The URLA has ten major sections, which are briefly described on pages 81–82.

As a rule, never sign any blank documents. After you have submitted your application, the lender will provide you with "Truth in Lending" information about your Annual Percentage Rate (APR) and the finance charge. You will also receive a "Good Faith Estimate" of your closing costs. These should be received within three business days of making the application. Chapter 6 explains the Truth in Lending; the Good Faith Estimate is covered in chapter 7.

AFTER YOU HAVE BEEN PRE-APPROVED

When you've been pre-approved, you'll get a pre-approval letter. This can be used during your negotiations with sellers. You'll also find that your sales agent will be even more committed. The letter demonstrates that you're a "real buyer" and not just "a looker." Be careful after you have been pre-approved. Don't go on a wild spending spree, lease a car, change your job, or do anything that can affect your credit. Remember, many lenders get a fresh report just before closing and will cancel your loan commitment if your

Universal Residential Loan Application

I. Type of Mortgage and Terms of Loan: Describe the type of loan you want.

II. Property Information and Purpose of Loan: Give the address and a legal description of the collateral. It asks if you are purchasing, refinancing, or building and whether the property is for a primary residence, secondary residence, or investment. Answers will determine the types of loans available. Terms are better if the property will be your primary residence. You may be asked for proof that you will be using the property as stated, especially if you own other properties. Indicate who will hold title and in which manner title is held. Chapter 5 addresses this issue.

III. Borrower Information: List personal information about yourself. If you have lived at the current address less than two years, you will need to list your previous addresses.

IV. Employment Information: List information about your present job. Also include additional employment history if you have worked elsewhere.

V. Monthly Income and Combined Housing Expense Information: Indicate your sources of income and major housing expenses, both present and proposed after you buy the house. The lender uses these numbers to calculate your "front ratio"(the percent of monthly income necessary to pay direct housing expenses, including mortgage payments).

VI. Assets and Liabilities: Indicate who holds your purchase deposit. List your savings and checking accounts, real estate, businesses owned, automobiles, and other assets. Indicate what you owe, including the remaining balance, monthly payments, and months left to pay. You must also indicate alimony owed and job-related expenses, such as union dues and child care. This is where the lender calculates the "back ratio" (the percent of monthly income necessary to

(continues)

(continued from page 81)

pay for direct housing expenses plus all long-term install-ment debt such as car payments). Before you fill out this sec-tion, see if you can reduce some of your time payments to less than ten months so they are not included. This will give you a better ratio and help out a lot on your loan approval.

VII. Details of Transaction: Indicate financial terms and closing costs. This shows you and the lender how much money you will have available to provide at closing.

VIII. Declarations: Declare bankruptcy and foreclosures within the past seven years, lawsuits, whether the down pay-ment is borrowed, your citizenship, and other information.

IX. Acknowledgment and Agreement: Make sure the in-formation on this form is accurate. In this section, you cer-tify all this information with your signature. If it is not cor-rect, you are subject to "civil liability and/or criminal penalties including, but not limited to, fine, or imprison-ment, or both." This is true even if the lender or your broker filled out the application, so check the application carefully.

X. Information for Government Monitoring Purposes: This is information about your race, national origin, and sex. It is optional on your part, but the lender is required to provide it to the government. Therefore, if you do not in-clude it, your loan officer will have to make her best guess on these factors.

credit becomes impaired. The loan is not final until your closing or settlement.

If you are pre-qualified and your loan is pre-approved, you have taken the fourth step. Congratulations!

4

Recruiting Your Dream Team

Y ou are now ready to hunt for your dream home. To help, you'll need to find some competent professionals whom you can trust to represent your best interests.

 ## THE SALES AGENT

One of the most important people you'll need is a good real estate broker or salesperson, referred to as "sales agent." A good sales agent is like a star quarterback on a championship team. If you don't select carefully, however, your quarterback could become a drawback. Why should you work with an agent? Consider the following experience of a couple who decided they didn't need a broker (with apologies to Norman Lear):

> Archie and Edith decided to buy a new home on their own. Actually, Archie decided.
> Edith asked, "Don't we need a broker, Archie?"
> Archie replied, "All real estate brokers are filthy cooks."
> "Don't you mean filthy crooks, Archie?"

"Stifle yourself, Edith! I know what I meant to say when I said what I didn't mean to say even if it sounded like I meant it."

With Archie's superior wisdom and communications skills, they drove out to the suburbs. They spotted a billboard offering new homes. Driving to a model home, a smooth-talking salesman named Eddie Haskell greeted them. He convinced them to buy the "Minnesota Fats Package," which included a wet bar, pool table, and Jacuzzi. This added 25% to the price. The builder provided the financing, which had a balloon payment due in five years. Two years after Archie and Edith moved in, their foundation cracked and a sinkhole opened in the backyard. The subdivision had been built on a landfill. When the balloon payment came due, the house was foreclosed. Archie and Edith had to move back to the city and rent a small apartment from their new landlords—George and Louise Jefferson.

> Most sales agents' primary goal is to earn the highest possible commission. Selling you the most expensive house you will buy is the means by which they reach their goal.

Most sales agents' primary goal is to earn the highest possible commission. Selling you the most expensive house you will buy is the means by which they reach their goal. In many cases, the sales agent represents the seller—not you. They want the highest price for their client rather than the lowest price for you, the buyer.

Some new sales agents know very little about real estate. After you've read this book, you'll probably know more about buying a house than most agents who just received their real estate licenses. The only reason these agents can get anything done is because they have experienced managers or brokers who supervise them.

Why Even Bother with an Agent?

You can probably find a house on your own. So you might think: Won't I save money by not having to pay the agent's commission? Although this may seem like a good idea, buyers who don't use an agent usually end up spending more money than if they had hired a good agent. Why is this? Even if you're not using an agent to buy your house, most of the sellers are. In fact, approximately 80% or more of the houses on the market are "listed" with real estate brokers. A listing means that the seller has signed a contract promising to pay the broker a commission if the house is sold during the listing period. The seller owes that commission even if the broker did not participate in selling the house! So you can't directly approach a seller who has signed a listing and try to buy the house and save on the commission.

> Buyers who don't use an agent usually end up spending more money than if they had hired a good agent.

Therefore, if you don't want to pay a commission, you are limited to houses that are "for sale by owner" (FSBOs). Will you save the amount of the commission by dealing with these sellers? Probably not. Many of these sellers are tightfisted. If they don't want to pay a commission to a broker, they certainly don't want to give you a price break. Furthermore, they might have overpriced the home and no reputable broker wanted to take the listing at that price. Now you might find the exact dream house you've been looking for, priced below market, offered by a seller willing to further reduce the price because no commission needs to be paid. If you're that lucky, you could probably win the Powerball lottery!

FINDING A GOOD SALES AGENT

So how do you find the best agent to help you? First, you want to find someone to represent *you, not the seller.* What's so hard about that? Can't you just go to an open house or call the agent who is advertising a house you want in the newspaper? No. In most states, brokers represent the seller unless the broker expressly agrees to represent the buyer. If the broker *or* his company has the house listed, he always represents the seller because of something called the Multiple Listing Service (MLS).

The MLS is an agreement among brokers to make available their listings to all other brokers. The broker with whom the seller has signed an "exclusive right to sell" is called the "listing broker." This person *always* represents the seller. This person is also entitled to the entire commission if the property is sold by anybody—even the seller—during the listing period.

The broker who brings the buyer to the transaction is called the "cooperating broker." According to the MLS agreement, the cooperating broker also represents the seller *unless* it is clearly stated that the cooperating broker is only representing the buyer. In most states, this requires a written buyer agency disclosure. Although the listing broker earns the whole commission if the house is sold, the MLS agreement states that the listing broker must share the commission with the cooperating broker.

Complications occur if a broker shows a house that is also listed by the same broker or her company. By definition, the broker represents the seller. The only way the broker can also represent the buyer is if he becomes a "dual agent." Both the seller and the buyer must agree to this change. A dual agent represents everybody and at the same time nobody. There is no earthly way he can negotiate the lowest price for you and at the same time negotiate the highest price for his other client, the seller. In other words, having a dual agent is like having no representation at all.

Don't some brokers work as "buyer's brokers"? Yes, but you may have to pay the broker directly. This fee could be paid hourly or based on a percentage of the sales price. However, in most states it's customary for the commission to be shared by the listing broker (representing the seller) and the buyer's broker (representing you). If you can't get the broker to both represent you and agree to be paid out of the sales price, keep looking for another agent. Remember, if you deal with a listing broker, she represents the seller and not you.

Some buyer's agents will try to get you to sign an exclusive contract for a long period of time, such as for six months. Don't do this. Instead, if you do sign a contract, limit the time to no more than one month. Your ability to find a new agent if the first one doesn't work out is a great motivator for your current agent to work quickly. Agents may also try to intimidate you into signing a printed "standard form." They may tell you that it's a standard contract that cannot be changed. Don't believe them. All contracts can be changed (as we'll talk about in chapter 5). Walk out and find another agent. By misstating the law, the agent shows that protecting her commission is more important than acting ethically in your best interest.

The only time you should consider paying your buyer's broker directly is when you are using her to buy from an FSBO. The fee to represent you is usually from 2% to 3% of the purchase price. If you want your agent to work harder at getting a lower price for you, here's a trade secret. Assume that an owner has a house listed for $220,000, and you will pay no more than $210,000 for it. This price is consistent with the value indicated by the Competitive Market Analysis (see chapter 5). Make a deal with your agent that for every $1 she is able to reduce the sales price under $210,000, you will pay her a bonus of 10%. If the house sells for $210,000, your agent earns a commission of $6,300 ($210,000 × 3% = $6,300). However, if the house sells for $200,000, your agent earns $7,000. This gives her a real incentive to try to get the seller to accept a lower price. Let's look at the math:

Commission on sales price	$200,000 × 3% = $6,000
Bonus on $10,000 savings	$10,000 × 10% = <u>1,000</u>
Total commission	= $7,000

Begin looking for a buyer's agent by asking friends who have had a good experience with their sales agents. Other real estate professionals such as mortgage lenders, escrow agents, insurance salespersons, title insurance officers, real estate attorneys, and appraisers are also good sources of leads. Check newspaper ads, the yellow pages, and the Internet for brokers who advertise that they represent buyers. Although you can try calling agents who have the most "For Sale" signs (especially those indicating "Sold") in neighborhoods in which you are interested, they may primarily be "listing agents" and not motivated or experienced in representing buyers. Finally, consider calling real estate offices near your target neighborhoods. Ask to talk to the "principal broker" (boss of the entire company) or broker in charge (boss of that office) and tell them you want an experienced agent to help you buy a home.

After you've assembled a list of names, contact the state real estate commission or the state office of consumer protection. Ask if any name on your list has had consumer complaints. The Better Business Bureau is another good way to check on agents.

Interviewing Agents

Call at least three of these candidates and ask for an interview. Although this can be done over the phone, it's preferable to make physical contact so you can judge the body language and demeanor of the candidates. If they can't make time to see you personally for an interview, they won't have time to help later when you really need them. Drop them from your list. During the interview with each candidate, try to determine whether he or she has any problems. Following is a list of typical problems you should look for, along with the questions you'll want to ask to make sure you

Complaints Against Brokers

The most common serious complaints against brokers and sales agents include the following:

1. Misrepresenting facts about the property (hidden or other defects like leaking roof or basement, asbestos, and so on)
2. Misrepresenting facts about off-site factors affecting property (zoning, building codes, property taxes, and so on)
3. Mishandling earnest money deposits
4. Disputes over contracts (drafting problems that could have been avoided if a lawyer had been used)
5. Violation of fair housing laws

choose the right agent. You can ask some questions over the phone; others are best answered in person.

PROBLEM: You will be entrusting a sales agent with a lot—your life savings and the commitment of paying from 25% to 40% of your future earnings for thirty years. You need a sales agent with integrity, a sense of ethics, and knowledge of the business. Anybody can become a real estate licensee once they pass a licensing exam; some also become REALTORS or Realtists. A REALTOR is a member of the National Association of REALTORS (NAR). This is a trade association with about 750,000 members. REALTORS subscribe to a Code of Ethics and pursue self-education in their field. Realtists are members of the National Association of Real Estate Brokers (NAREB). The NAREB Web site states: "Although composed principally of African

American and other minority real estate professionals, the organization is an integrated entity open to all qualified practitioners. . . ." Some sales agents are members of both organizations.

QUESTION TO ASK: "Do you belong to a real estate trade or professional organization?"

ANSWER YOU WANT: "Yes, I am a REALTOR." Or, "Yes, I am a Realtist."

PROBLEM: Can or will the agent represent you? As mentioned earlier, in most states brokers automatically represent the seller unless it is made clear, in writing, that they will represent the buyer exclusively. If the agent's firm has the listing, it is legally impossible to give you exclusive representation. At best she can take on the role of "dual" agent. Because this is never a good idea, you will need to get another agent to represent you for that specific house. Based on a current survey by the National Association of REALTORS, 8% of REALTORS practice only buyer agency, 13% practice only seller agency, whereas 19% practice single agency representing either the buyer or seller but not both. However, an overwhelming 53% practice dual agency. This means that most sales agents will want you to accept them as dual agents, giving up any representation whatsoever. Because they do this to keep the entire commission rather than sharing it, they are unlikely to want to cut into their commission by getting you a lower price. Avoid becoming a victim. Don't accept a dual agency!

QUESTION TO ASK: "Will you be able to act as my exclusive agent, and are you willing to put this commitment into writing?"

ANSWER YOU WANT: "Yes." The candidate can explain the issue of houses listed with her firm and the possibility of dual agency. Let the agent know that for those houses you will use a different agent to ensure exclusive representation. How they react to this is important. If they argue about it, walk out. They will probably be hard to work with in the future. You want an agent who will represent your best interest, not their own.

PROBLEM: Is the candidate experienced in the real estate industry? The business is easy to enter. It is also easy to drop out of it. Most new licensees leave the business after two years, usually because they still don't know how to properly serve their clients professionally. In 1999, 19% of REALTORS had less than three years of experience.

> In most states, brokers automatically represent the seller unless it is made clear, in writing, that they will represent the buyer exclusively.

QUESTION TO ASK: "How many years have you been in the real estate brokerage business?"

ANSWER YOU WANT: You want to hear at least three years. Five years of experience is much better. Get the pros working for you and hope that the rookies are representing the seller.

PROBLEM: Does the agent work full or part time? Full-timers treat the job as a profession. They are serious about their field and are likely to be much better informed. On the other hand, most part-timers treat the job as a hobby. They don't have the time to preview newly listed houses or to stay informed about things vital to your decision. Nationwide, approximately 40% of REALTORS work fewer than 40 hours per week, and 12% work fewer than 20 hours per week.

QUESTION TO ASK: "Are you a full-time or part-time real estate agent?"

ANSWER YOU WANT: "Full-time." Or better, "I work 24/7 at this business."

PROBLEM: The National Association of REALTORS reports that about 87% of all REALTORS have at least some college education. Only 13% have a high school education or less. Generally, the more education the sales agent has, the more likely they will be to serve you. Note that a formal education is not as important as specific courses in real estate subjects and local area knowledge, but it helps.

QUESTION TO ASK: "How much formal education have you completed?"

ANSWER YOU WANT: "I have a college degree from XYZ State University."

PROBLEM: Some states have very few requirements to become a sales agent. Most are limited to taking a course lasting about one week and then passing a real estate exam. Some agents are fortunate enough to work for a real estate firm with a good training program. Others work hard to take additional courses from a real estate professional organization. These are the agents you want. They have worked to gain additional knowledge in their field and show commitment. This is particularly true if they have earned certain professional designations to certify their competency.

QUESTION TO ASK: "Do you have any profession designations? If so, which ones?"

ANSWERS YOU WANT:

"Yes, I have the GRI designation." (GRI means "Graduate, REALTORS Institute). From 15% to 25% of all REALTORS have taken a series of courses (the equivalent of three college courses) and passed exams to get this designation.

"Yes, I have the ABR designation." Or, "Yes, I have the ABRM designation." About 6% of REALTORS have the ABR (Accredited Buyer Representative) awarded by the Real Estate Buyer's Agent Council (REBAC). To gain this designation, the agent must take a two-day course and have five transactions in which he represented buyers within 36 months of passing the course. The ABRM (Accredited Buyer Representative Manager) requires an additional course with a second elective course as well.

"Yes, I have the CRS designation." Or, "Yes, I have the CRB designation." NAR statistics indicate that about 12% have the CRS (Certified Residential Specialist), requiring them to sell at least seventy-five homes during a five-year period and take several courses. About 3% have the CRB (Certified Residential Brokerage Manager). These agents usually have the CRS and must meet additional education requirements.

PROBLEMS: How experienced and successful is this agent? How familiar is the agent in representing buyers? Is he familiar with the houses in the neighborhood in which you are interested? You will have to judge the answers for yourself.

QUESTIONS TO ASK

"Do you primarily represent buyers or sellers?"

"How many buyers are you currently helping?"

"How many sellers are you currently helping?"

"Can you work in my time frame?"

"How can I contact you if I need help? Are you available to work at night? On weekends?"

"Are you familiar with homes selling in XYZ neighborhood(s)?"

"How many homes have you sold overall?"

"How many homes have you sold in XYZ neighborhood(s)?"

"What is the average price of the homes you help people buy?"

"Have you won any sales awards from your company?"

"Will you be able to provide me with a Competitive Market Analysis when the time comes for me to make a serious offer?"

"What other services do you provide?"

"Will you advise me if any houses I look at have problems, either in the house or in the surrounding area?"

"Will you be able to research the answer to any question I have about a house or the neighborhood? For example, can you provide me with sales statistics or zoning or deed restrictions?"

"Will you be able to advise me about any other real estate experts I may need and recommend whom I might need to hire?"

"Can you give me the names and numbers of three buyers you've helped and whom I can call as references?"

FINAL QUESTION: "Can you recommend an experienced agent at another company to represent me?"

ANSWER YOU WANT: This can be the clincher. Watch the agent's body language and expression. Do they forthrightly suggest someone because they are concerned about your best interest, or are they suddenly concerned about themselves and losing a possible commission. This question tests the candidate's integrity.

Trying Out the Agent

After the interview, call at least three buyers who have worked with the agent. Ask if they were happy with their representation? Ask how successfully the agent solved their problems.

After you have selected your best choice, test the agent out by having her show you one house. Be sure to give her a copy of your HOME PROFILE in advance. Did the agent find a house that met your needs, or did she just take you to a convenient place she had listed? How professionally does she act? Is she on time? Is her car clean or messy? How carefully does she listen to you and answer your questions. Is she pushy? Is she helpful? How committed is she in helping you find exactly what you need and want. Most important, will you and your spouse be comfortable working with this person?

Even though an agent may seem sincere, trustworthy, and competent, you should still take the following precautions to protect yourself:

1. Don't be afraid to ask questions and demand direct and factual answers.

2. Whenever possible, cross-check the answers, especially if the original answer doesn't quite make sense or your intuition tells you that something seems wrong.

3. Do your homework. Know what you want, where you need to live, and how much you want to pay.

4. Familiarize yourself with the market (chapter 3 provides practical suggestions on how to do this).

5. Keep some information secret. Don't reveal everything to your sales agent. No matter how friendly the agent is, don't assume she is your friend. Make friends after you've moved into your new home.

6. Don't be afraid to ask questions and demand direct and factual answers. (Yes, this is listed twice because it is very important).

7. Do your own research; don't depend exclusively on what the agent or others tell you.

8. Don't be pressured or intimidated. You are making a very big decision and may need additional time to think or talk things over with your spouse—away from your agent.

9. Don't be afraid to terminate your relationship and find a new sales agent.

10. Don't be afraid to work with more than one agent if necessary. This is important if the first agent is not familiar with neighborhoods you are considering or if the agent does not belong to all MLS services in town (some cities have more than one service). Also, you will definitely need another agent if the house you want to buy is listed by the first agent's company.

What to Expect from Your Agent

At this point, you may be asking yourself why it's necessary to invest so much time and effort in finding a good agent. A good agent can help you find a better house faster and for a better price than you can ordinarily find for yourself. On the other hand, a bad agent can misdirect you, waste your time, cause you to overpay for a house, and leave you with years of regret.

The services a good agent provides include:

- *Information.* A good agent knows about local market conditions, planning and zoning information, schools, shopping, transportation service, and other facts that may affect your life as well as the future value of the home. She will also warn you about dangers such as local flooding conditions, future developments such as roadwork that can affect the neighborhood, proposed property tax increases, and special assessments. The agent may also share local knowledge about termites, sliding or other unstable soil conditions, and impassible conditions during ice or snowstorms. For example, in the Dallas-Fort Worth area, many residents must "water their foundations" so the hot summer heat does not cause them to crack as the clay soil shrinks or expands.

- *Investigation.* A good agent can investigate public records for information about the property. She can access computer databases for market prices and trends and other information to help you prepare an offer based on a reasonable price.

- *Inspection.* A good agent can inspect the house, yard, and off-site features to warn you about quality problems and red flags that indicate the need for professional inspections, surveys, or further disclosures from the seller.
- *Negotiation.* A good agent can negotiate the contract on your behalf to get you a better price, better terms, and other concessions. She should be an experienced negotiator. It helps considerably if your agent has a lot of experience on the job.

> A good agent can help you find a better house, faster, and for a better price than you can ordinarily find it for yourself.

- *Recommendation.* A good agent can recommend other members for your team, such as home inspectors, surveyors, lenders, movers, insurance agents, repair contractors, interior decorators, and other service providers.
- *Coordination.* A good agent coordinates all activities that take place after the contract is signed and before closing. This includes resolving any incomplete contract contingencies, the provision of services (such as surveys or repairs), the completion of all necessary paperwork, the final inspections, and, of course, the walk-through.
- *Mediation.* A good agent can mediate and resolve disputes as well as help solve problems that occur during the process. For example, what if you discover that the neighbor's rock wall is encroaching over the boundary or an existing rental tenant refuses to leave? Or what if the seller balks over personal property he agreed to include? You probably won't know what to do, but a good agent will.

BEGINNING THE SEARCH

Once you have an agent, you are ready to begin your search for the perfect home. Give a copy of your HOME PROFILE (figure 2.2 in chapter 2) and your list of the target neighborhoods to your agent. Be sure to go through the profile with your agent, explaining all your needs and wants. Make sure she understands what you are looking for so she doesn't waste time searching for homes you won't want. Although you need to indicate the price range, keep the absolute highest amount to yourself. Always try to start out low. Then if you don't like the type or quality of houses, you can always increase the upper limit of the price range. Many agents will usually look at the high end of your price range because their commission depends on the price you pay.

Your agent will take your HOME PROFILE and do a computer search of all houses on the MLS that meet your specifications. Sit down with the agent and locate each house on your map. Be sure to label the houses on the map for quick and easy identification. For example, you may label the first house as "A," the second as "B," and so forth. Now you and your agent need to take a look at these homes. The agent will make appointments for you to see each. Because some houses have "lock-boxes" outside with the key to the house, you can usually see them without an appointment. However, when homes are still occupied by the owner or a tenant, you may have to wait a couple of days for an appointment.

Keeping Score

Most people, after visiting several houses, begin to suffer from information overload. All the homes begin to blur together, and you can't remember the specifics of each house. In fact, you may find yourself arguing with your spouse about which house had this or that. You need some way to keep track of each home and identify how it compares to your dream home.

"The Profile Score of Home Offered," shown in figure 4.1, is a great way to evaluate each home you visit and record your opinions. The score for each home is based on your HOME PROFILE. The closer the house matches your profile, the higher the score. The form also allows you to include features you hadn't considered on your profile. For example, a home might have a built-in barbecue and fire pit in the backyard. Although you did not list this as a want, because you really like it, you can give the home some bonus points. The form also includes an adjustment for the overall quality of the home.

You should visit and examine each home your agent has identified as coming close to your profile. Take pictures of each home to help you remember it. I recommend using a digital camera so you can view your shots quickly rather than wait to have them developed. Take a clipboard along during each visit so you can take notes on the Profile Score, making a judgment and listing a score for each feature you feel is important. You can add up the scores later. Once you have checked out all of the homes, lay out your Profile scores along with the accompanying photos. Now compare the scores and narrow your choices down to the top three. Take a drive past these finalists, then select the house you consider your best buy.

Let your agent know that you would like to make an offer on the house you selected. However, before making an actual offer, you need to obtain from the seller a written disclosure of the property condition. Most states currently make this disclosure mandatory. Within it, the seller must disclose all serious defects in the house. Most disclosure forms are a detailed checklist of features in the house. During your preliminary inspection, you will want to carefully scrutinize those features highlighted.

Your agent will need to collect additional information on your behalf from the public records, from the Community Association (if there is one), and from the seller. Items such

Figure 4.1 **Profile Score Of Home Offered**

Address: _____

Asking price: _____

Brief description: _____

_____

_____

Listing Agent

Name: _____

Company: _____

Telephone: _____ **Fax:** _____ **E-Mail:** _____

(Note: Attach photo or indicate number on digital camera.)

Needs	Wants and Maximum Points to be Awarded for Each Extra Feature	Comments About the Quality and Condition of Feature and Other Information	Bonus Points Awarded
3 bedrooms	Extra bedroom: 5 points		
2 full baths	½ bath: 5 points; 1 full extra bath: 10 points		
	Walk-in closet in master bedroom: 3 points		

Kitchen with eating area — Formal dining room: 5 points

Family room — Formal living room: 5 points

House size: At least 2,000 square feet — More space: 1 point for each extra 100 square feet

Attic storage space — Finished attic: 10 points

Basement storage space — Finished basement: 5 points

Laundry

Carport — 2-car garage: 5 points; 3-car garage: 8 points

Lot at least 30,000 square feet — More land: 1 point for each additional 2,000 square feet

Dishwasher: 2 points

Disposal: 1 point

Fireplace: 2 points

Modern electrical wiring: 10 points

Backyard deck: 3 points

Age of house — Less than 3 years: 10 points; Less than 5 years: 5 points; 10 years or less: 3 points; minus 1 for each year older than 10 years

Swimming pool: 2 points

Location in neighborhood — Excellent: 5 points; Good: 3 points

(continues)

Figure 4.1 Profile Score Of Home Offered (continued)

Needs	Wants and Maximum Points to be Awarded for Each Extra Feature	Comments About the Quality and Condition of Feature and Other Information	Bonus Points Awarded
View	Excellent: 5 points; Good: 3 points		
	Security system: 2 points		
Neighborhood A			15 points

Other Features

1.

2.

3.

Quality Score

Perfect: 25 points; Excellent: 20 points; Very Good: 15 points; Good: 10 points; Poor: minus 10; Fixer upper: minus 25 points

TOTAL SCORE: _____

ADDITIONAL COMMENTS: _____

as utility bills will help you estimate a budget for your monthly living expenses. Next, both you and your agent need to make a preliminary inspection. If you don't like what you read in the seller's disclosure statement or what you find during the inspection, go to your next home choice or ask your agent to show you more houses. You might want to consider some more expensive homes as well as FSBOs.

PRELIMINARY INSPECTION OF THE HOUSE

During your inspection, be sure to make a list of problems and identify any red flags you discover. Give a copy of this list to your professional inspector for additional investigation and his estimate of probable repair costs. You should then use this information to adjust your offering price or during negotiation with the seller.

When you go to inspect, dress in long pants, long-sleeved washable shirt, and practical shoes with a good grip. You will poke around in the attic, the basement, and in other dusty or dirty areas of the house. Bring along a camera (with a flash), a flashlight, a penknife, binoculars, level, measuring tape, a notepad, and pencil. Also, bring a plug-in nightlight to test the electrical outlets. If blueprints and a lot plan are available, take those as well.

Off-Site and Neighborhood Conditions to Investigate

Many buyers, agents, and home inspectors focus only on the structural aspects of the building and ignore off-site and neighborhood characteristics that impact the quality of life. Be sure to look at these items during your inspection and take notes as needed.

1. In new developments, have the streets been dedicated to the local government? If not, you and your neighbors may be financially liable for maintaining these and have additional liability if someone is hurt because of defective design.

Timely Inspection

Inspect the house at different times of the day and, if possible, under different weather conditions. Let me share two personal examples to illustrate why this is important: I was interested in oceanfront property that was shown to me at high tide. The view from the outdoor balcony was wonderful. Later, as I was trying to determine my offer, I drove to the property without the agent. I was shocked to see an ugly mudflat extending hundreds of yards out from the property at low tide.

In another case, my agent called to suggest we examine a condominium on which I had made an offer. She thought I should see it in the rain. When we arrived, we surprised the listing broker and his wife, who were busily mopping up and trying to conceal water damage caused by roof leaks. Because of this, we adjusted my offer by $10,000 to close the deal. Later I replaced the carpeting, had the rooms repainted, and the leaks fixed for about $2,500.

2. Are there nearby schools, stadiums, highways, railroad tracks, or airports that can create excessive noise? Be sure to walk all the way into the backyard and around the neighborhood. As you do, look, listen, and smell.

3. What are the plans for the adjoining, empty tracts of land? Do city plans and zoning allow these to be developed into incompatible land uses, such as factories or warehouses?

4. Is the property in a flood plain? If so, what will flood insurance cost? Is there a stream or wetlands nearby

that isn't visible from the property but may affect it after a heavy rain?

5. Is the air or water quality affected by nearby polluting industries or a Superfund site? Is the groundwater contaminated from leaking underground storage tanks or buried wastes, including buried vegetation that can cause methane gas contamination? The state department of environmental protection or department of health may have records indicating nearby landfills, gas stations, industrial uses, and other sources of toxic problems.

6. Where is the property located within the neighborhood? Is it on a street with heavy traffic or on a quiet cul-de-sac? Is it a corner lot with a great deal of grass to mow and reduced privacy, or is it in the center of the block? Is it next to a noisy school or next to a quiet, scenic park?

Site Conditions to Investigate

House inspectors and engineers seldom consider problems involving the lot. You and your agent should take time to examine the lot for possible problems. A surveyor can identify some problems like encroachments and other boundary line issues.

1. If possible, get a certified survey from sellers showing the property boundaries. There may have been verbal errors misrepresenting lot size or boundaries.

Helpful Hint

The EPA has a good Web site listing neighborhood hazards in many different areas throughout the country. Before considering a neighborhood, especially in an area with which you are unfamiliar, review this site.

www.epa.gov/epahome
/commsearch.htm

Type in the zip code of the home you're considering and find out about businesses that use toxic substances in the area as well as other possible dangers.

2. Look at the drainage. Improperly drained water can be very destructive. Does water pool in areas, creating breeding grounds for mosquitoes?

3. What is the age and condition of the trees? Do they have problems with borers or poisonous insects? Large, dead trees are expensive to remove.

4. Does the lot contain dangers such as wells that have been improperly capped by rotting boards?

5. What is on the other side of the boundary? Is there a railroad track? Do your neighbors keep chicken or pigs? Is there a large forest that you later discover is zoned for commercial or industrial uses?

6. Does a nearby brook or stream cause worry about flooding? Does a nearby lake lead to worry about alligators in the deep South or water snakes in other parts of the country?

7. If you plan to build a tennis court or other improvement, do you have enough land? Has your agent checked the zoning and deed restrictions?

8. If the property includes a swimming pool, has an expert checked it out?

9. Does something smell bad? Check it out. You may have a defective septic tank system.

House Conditions to Investigate

Both the exterior and interior of the house need to be examined. Do this systematically, room by room. Check insulation and ventilation, the condition of paint, any buckling or separation of wood, cracks in bricks or concrete, as well as evidence of proper, or improper, maintenance.

1. Walk around the exterior of the building and look at the areas near the foundation where the exterior wall meets the ground. Look for cracks and rot. Poke your penknife in the wood, especially where you find sawdust. Look for peeling paint. Look for shifting bricks or repairs that suggest that the entire wall has cracked or shifted. Examine boards for any curling away from the house. Examine gutters for rust or holes. Be concerned when you see plants growing out of the gutters. Use binoculars to examine the roof for shingles that are curling or cracked. If the roof is over twenty years old, it may need an expensive replacement. Inspect the chimney for cracked bricks. Poke your knife in the wood surrounding the windows to see whether you detect any rot. Measure the exterior dimensions of the house. Take notes of all your findings.

2. If possible, crawl under the house with your flashlight. You don't want to run into vermin such as skunks, rats, or snakes). Or go into the basement if the house has one. Check the condition of the pipes. Look for stains or sawdust. Take notes on any problems you see. You are looking primarily for foundation or shifting problems. For very old houses, those classics that were built near the beginning of the twentieth century, worry about packed coal under the floor or abandoned gas pipes. Also check for evidence that the basement floods (water stains, a smell or feeling of dampness). You will definitely want a professional assessment if you see signs of any of these problems.

3. Go inside. How easily do the doors and windows open? Defective windows are expensive to replace. Use a level to check the floors.

4. Go into the kitchen and ask which appliances are included. Check those and ask if these are still under

warranty. Identify any existing owner's manuals for all equipment in the house.

5. Go into all bathrooms. Are there enough for your family? Examine the age and condition of all bathroom fixtures. Test the water pressure by turning on all water faucets and flushing the toilet. Taste the water from the sink tap. Consider taking a water sample and having it tested.

6. Go into each room and measure it.

7. Look at, but don't touch, the electrical wiring and the fuse or circuit box. Is the system at least 100-amp? Is there a 220-amp line for the washer, dryer, and range? Do any of the lights flicker or not work. You can pick up a tester at a hardware store to check each electrical outlet or use a cheaper plug-in nightlight to be sure all work. Your professional home inspector will check out the electrical systems more completely.

8. Check heating, air-conditioning, hot water heater, and other systems. How old are these. Your professional inspector will give a more in-depth evaluation.

9. Go into the attic with your flashlight and look for water stains. Watch out for bats or bird nests. If you want to add a room in the attic, is it high enough?

10. Stop and take some time in each room to imagine you and your family using it.

Red Flags Indicating Possible Health Hazards

Although most problems can be corrected, some hazards cannot be resolved no matter how much money you spend. Houses that contain unsolvable problems that can affect the

Radon Warning

Radon, an odorless, colorless gas that comes primarily from radiation within the soil, is responsible for more lung cancer deaths than any other cause except smoking. Radon primarily affects buildings that are sealed for energy efficiency. It comes from cracks in solid floors, cracks in walls, and cavities inside walls and intrudes into enclosed spaces, building up to dangerous levels. It is easy and cheap to test for and correct. Ask for the home to be radon-tested by a qualified tester, unless you like the odds (harmful levels of radon are found in one out of every fifteen houses). Your agent must advise you if radon is a problem in the area. Red flags include pet birds shedding feathers and sellers who seem to have respiratory problems. The cause might not be a cold or flu, but a sick building.

health and safety of your family should be avoided entirely. Some hazards are potentially deadly.

1. If a house if offered "as is," big red flags should be waving all over in your mind. By offering the house "as is," the seller realizes that the market will expect a huge price discount. The only reason a seller would accept such a price reduction is because he knows something is seriously wrong with his property.

2. Indoor air quality can cause serious health problems. A legislative committee in one northern state concluded that 50% of all illnesses result from indoor air pollution. Common forms of indoor air pollution include carbon monoxide, mold spores, and radon.

Energy-efficient homes built after 1970 are often troubled by these problems because their heavy insulation and well-sealed doors and windows allow harmful toxins to build up. Old carpeting and draperies suffer from "outgassing" as materials begin to decay or accumulate mold. Look for black spots on the wall. A deadly mold problem could be lurking behind those walls.

3. Beware of odd or suspicious details when you inspect a house—especially those that suggest a "cover-up." Are some rooms closed so you can't get in, even if you ask? Is the seller keeping all windows open or burning incense? Are air fresheners positioned throughout the house? Does the smell indicate that air fresheners were used recently? Are selected parts of the house painted, and does the paint smell fresh? Are heavy furniture or other large objects pushed against the wall—perhaps covering up something?

4. Do you see or smell evidence of decay or bug infestation. For example, do you smell mildew? Do you see piles of sawdust in the attic or basement?

5. Beware of lead paint in houses built prior to 1978.

6. Stay away from houses that have underground oil storage tanks.

 ## PROFESSIONAL INSPECTION OF THE HOUSE

Many years ago, I was asked to draft legislation for my home state's seller disclosure law and the licensing law for home inspectors. I ran a number of experiments comparing the effectiveness of licensed sales agents and a professional home inspector in finding defects. The home inspector found two to three times as many defects as the sales agents. In fact, the real estate agents totally missed some serious defects. Ever since my experiment, I have consistently recommended using professional home inspectors or engineers.

In some markets, sellers have already had the house inspected and use the inspection as a marketing tool. However, don't rely on those inspections. Pay to have your own inspection done, especially if your preliminary inspection has identified red flags. Normally, a house isn't professionally inspected until after the contract is signed. The contract will include a contingency that the sale is subject to the completion of a satisfactory inspection. If I am serious about purchasing a house, I like to get the inspection completed as early as possible, unless there is not enough time or other buyers are interested in the house. A completed inspection report can be used during the negotiation to reduce the price and/or have repairs done.

Selecting an Inspector or Engineer

Many states license home inspectors. If possible, use a state-licensed inspector who is also a member of the American Society of Home Inspectors (ASHI). Members of this organization agree to use ASHI's Standards of Practice. Also consider using professional engineers. Although they typically are more expensive, most have more engineering knowledge and experience necessary for complicated inspections. If you've found red flags suggesting serious problems, it's best to hire the engineer.

> **Helpful Hint**
>
> Both the American Society of Home Inspectors and the National Society of Professional Engineers maintain Web sites where you can find information on their members in your area. You can find their respective Web sites at:
>
> www.ashi.org
>
> www.nspe.org

Review the scope of the inspector's or the engineer's proposed inspection. Show him your list of problems and red flags identified during the preliminary inspection. If you have concerns about lead paint, asbestos, polybutylene pipe, or EIFS synthetic stucco (the last two have been subject to national class action lawsuits), be sure to have these included in the scope of the report. Also ask the inspector to estimate the repair cost of discovered defects. You will need this information for negotiating with the seller.

Most inspections are visual only and do not include destructive testing such as cutting holes into walls. However, if this type of testing is required, your agent needs to obtain written permission from the seller. Ask the inspector if you can accompany him on the inspection and whether you can photograph or videotape some of the problems he finds. Not only will you learn a lot about the house from an inspector, but also he will often provide suggestions on fixing problems and improving or modernizing functional problems. Don't forget to ask for a written report. Although this costs more than a verbal report, it is well worth it.

If you have selected and inspected your house, you have taken the fifth step. Congratulations!

Making the Deal Real

To finalize your purchase, you'll need to sign a contract that protects your rights and defines your obligations. A good contract is the result of an effective negotiation strategy. That strategy begins even before you see the house. Negotiation begins with your family agreeing to wants and needs. It continues when you select your agent and agree on whom she represents. You are even negotiating when you first walk into the house. What you say and the body language you use can signal the strength or weakness of your bargaining position.

Let's look at how a couple lost their negotiation when they first walked into an "open house" and then made even more mistakes after that.

Antony and Cleopatra were looking for a home. They saw an open house sign and stopped to look. Mr. J. Caesar greeted them and showed the features of the home. He heard Cleopatra tell Antony that she really loved the home and had to have it.

"What is the house worth?" asked Antony.

"At least as much as the listing price, and possibly more," Caesar replied. He then mentioned that a couple named Pompey indicated they were making a full-price offer that afternoon. Caesar then handed Antony and Cleopatra a "standard form contract" and urged them to make an offer for $1,000 more than the listing price if they didn't want to lose it to the Pompey couple. The contract consisted of many pages of fine print.

"There is no need to read it," Caesar told Antony and Cleopatra. "It's just standard language everyone uses." They signed the contract. However, at the settlement they discovered that they had agreed to pay all closing costs and to buy the house in "as is" condition. Later, they met their new neighbors, the Pompeys, who bought a house exactly like theirs for $50,000 less.

CONTRACT NEGOTIATION STRATEGY

A good real estate negotiation strategy requires both preparation and realistic expectations. This chapter presents the following step-by-step strategy:

1. Learn local rules and customs about how contracts are made. Understand standard forms that are used.

2. Find a competent real estate attorney to give you advice and review your contract.

3. Determine local market conditions such as whether you are dealing in a normal market or one that favors buyers or sellers.

4. Use a CMA (Competitive Market Analysis, see discussion on page 121) to estimate a fair value range for your target house.

5. Discover the seller's motivations and needs in order to judge his bargaining strength.

6. Make an initial offer based on how realistic the seller's listing price is and on factors that influence the seller's bargaining power.

7. Work through a broker's agent whom you trust, or consider a face-to-face negotiation.

8. Choose an appropriate negotiation style.

9. Make sure you negotiate all issues that affect your requirements or concerns.

10. Have your attorney review the final contract before you sign it.

 ## IMPORTANT REAL ESTATE CONTRACT CONCEPTS

Before we get into negotiating, let's quickly look at the contract you'll be negotiating. Names for real estate contracts vary throughout the country. They can be called Real Estate Purchase Contract; Contract of Sale; Purchase Offer; Purchase and Sales Agreement; Deposit Receipt, Offer and Acceptance; Earnest Money Receipt, Offer and Acceptance; Land Contract; Contract for Deed; Agreement of Sale; Option; and other various combinations of these words.

> ### Helpful Hint
> Don't sign a contract until you read it and fully understand what it means. Have your own attorney read the contract and advise you of legal pitfalls.

All real estate contracts must be written and must include every promise the seller or the seller's representative makes to you. Oral promises cannot be enforced. It's important to understand that a contract need not be written on a standard form. You can create a contract by writing on a placemat, the back of an envelope, or even a receipt—as long as these contain the essential elements. Local customs concerning contracts differ greatly throughout the United States. For example, in some parts of the country, buyers and sellers sign binders, which are essentially temporary agreements binding the two parties until an attorney drafts a more complete contract. If the binder has all the necessary elements of a contract, it is considered a contract and you are bound by it.

A real estate contract has six essential elements:

1. Date of contract
2. Identification of the buyer and seller
3. The agreement to buy and sell
4. Proper legal description of property
5. Price and terms
6. Signatures of the seller and buyer (in some states only the person being sued has to have signed)

If a document has all these essential elements, it's a contract. Most buyers and sellers include many more elements to completely explain and record each of their agreements. Following is a list of additional elements that should be included:

1. Time and place of closing
2. Who has the risk of loss between signing of contract and settlement
3. Amount of earnest money
4. Type of deed
5. Any warranties made by seller
6. Provisions for seller financing if the buyer can't borrow from a conventional lender or needs a second mortgage loan from the seller
7. Any agreements concerning personal property and fixtures

8. Any reservations or exceptions (that is, what the seller will not include or retains the rights to, such as an easement to keep crossing your land)
9. Contingencies
10. Prorations (adjustments at closing for insurance, property taxes, fuel in tank, and so on)
11. Whether "time is of the essence" (that is, whether terms will be strictly enforced)
12. What happens if there is a default

WHY YOU NEED A LAWYER

The items above are just a partial list of provisions that might need to be included. Unless you are an attorney, you may leave yourself wide open to unexpected legal disasters. For example, consider the following contract:

July 15, 2001

John Doe (seller) agrees to sell to Mary Smith (buyer) who agrees to buy the house and property known as Lot 23, Block C of XYZ subdivision for $200,000. A deposit receipt of $10,000 cash is acknowledged. Closing is at noon on September 5, 2001.

John Doe (Seller)   *Mary Smith* (Buyer)

Is this a valid contract? It may or may not be. July 15, 2001, fell on a Sunday. Some states do not recognize contracts signed on Sundays. What happens if Mary Smith cannot get financing? She will lose her $10,000 and can even be sued for breach of contract because the contract has no financing contingency to protect her. What happens if the house burns down on August 1, 2001? Can Mary cancel the deal because the house is destroyed? The answer is unclear. Under common law, she already has equitable ownership of the house because the contract has no conditions. Mary could suffer

Lawyer Listing: www.martindale.com

Martindale-Hubble maintains a Web site listing all types of lawyers and allows you to narrow them down by specialty and city. At the homepage, click the "Location/Area of Practice" tab. Under "Select general area of practice," select "Real Estate" and then type in the city and state. You will then be given a list of real estate attorneys in the area. Select a lawyer and click on "Rating Info" to see how the lawyer is rated by other attorneys. Only 43% of lawyers are rated. This site also lists attorneys fluent in other languages for buyers who do not speak English.

the loss because the contract doesn't address the issue of which party has the risk of loss before closing. Some states have special laws that cover this situation.

Are you beginning to see the importance of a lawyer in protecting your rights?

Use of lawyers varies throughout the country. In some states such as New York, use of attorneys is essential. In other states, attorneys are seldom used because most transactions use standard form contracts with addenda that can be mechanically filled in by real estate brokers. However, in many of these situations, buyers are at risk because a qualified real estate attorney is not there to protect their interests.

It's a very good idea to have an attorney on your team. How do you find one? Referrals from friends, other real estate professionals, and the state bar association are good sources. One national company called Martindale-Hubble lists and classifies most of the attorneys in this country by their area of practice.

THE ART OF NEGOTIATION

Preparing for negotiation involves several things—understanding market conditions, the actual market value of the property, the relative strength and motivation of the seller, and even your ability to control your emotions. It also includes using an agent properly and developing an approach designed to maximize your strengths while minimizing your weaknesses.

Is It a Seller's or Buyer's Market?

As a buyer, your ability to negotiate a better price will be based on the current market, which might include an entire community or be limited to one or two neighborhoods. Markets are usually normal; however, some are considered "seller's markets" and others "buyer's markets." According to economists, price is determined by supply and demand. Sellers (supply) and buyers (demand) establish the value in a real estate market. They make offers and counteroffers to find a price that will yield a sale. These offers are based on what the parties hope is the least money a seller will accept and the most money a buyer will pay and often consider what people have paid in the past for similar properties. Factors influencing value include scarcity of product; numbers of people seeking to buy; location, quality, and amenity differences; and a broad range of personal considerations. That's why some real estate markets are hot, while others are not.

Let's look at the factors that influence prices:

1. **Supply and demand.** When supply is low and demand is high, prices tend to increase. When supply is high and demand is low, prices tend to decrease.

2. **Interest rates.** Lowering interest rates will mean increased demand, whereas rising rates will do the opposite.

3. **Building permits.** Builders are constantly forecasting home markets. When newspapers report an increase in building permits, this can mean that a supply shortage is expected and prices will be going up. It also can mean that builders are over building and prices may go down. You have to consider all of the factors to decide what an increase in building permits means.

4. **Home sales trends.** Your broker's agent can supply MLS sales statistics. If there is a great spread between listing price and actual selling price, and if inventories are increasing over a nine- or ten-month supply, this is a sign of a buyer's market. But if the spread is narrow and inventory is below a five-month supply, this is a sign of a seller's market.

> When supply is low and demand is high, prices tend to increase. When supply is high and demand is low, prices tend to decrease.

5. **Foreclosure sales.** When the number of foreclosures increases, this is a sign that the market is weakening and prices are, or soon will be, soft, which could be good for buyers. Soft prices mean that sellers will be more willing to make price concessions.

6. **Seasonal influence.** Sellers can get better prices if they are marketing their houses in the spring and summer. Most buyers are looking in the spring and summer so that they can make their moves while school is out. Buyers, on the other hand, have the strongest bargaining power in late fall and winter. But who wants to move in the winter? Often, the houses on the winter market suffer from deficiencies that prevented a sale during the better selling season.

The nature of the market will influence your strategy. In a seller's market, you will often be in a race to buy a house before the price goes up. Brokers will be impatient with buyers who are too aggressive in trying to get lower prices. However, in a buyer's market, sellers are often willing to make dramatic concessions to get you to buy, and brokers may go out of their way to accommodate your whims. The negotiation strategy described in this chapter is designed for normal markets. However, it can be adjusted for other types of markets as well.

Helpful Hint

You can be a tough negotiator in a buyer's market, but this strategy will backfire in a seller's market.

Competitive Market Analysis (CMA)

Before you can make an informed offer, you need to know what the house is worth. A very helpful tool for determining this is the CMA. Depending on where you live, CMA stands for "Competitive Market Analysis," "Comparative Market Analysis," or "Comparable Market Analysis." Listing agents prepare a CMA for sellers who are their clients, and this is the basis of the seller's listing price and negotiation strategy. Most listing agents will not provide this information to you. However, if you work with a buyer's agent, she can easily get you your own CMA.

The CMA is a very crude form of an appraisal. Recent sales of similar houses in the same market or neighborhood, called "comparables" or "comps," are listed. However, CMAs are not standard. Their information depends on who prepares them. For example, a CMA prepared by a listing agent is almost always biased toward the high side of the price scale. Even a CMA prepared by a buyer's agent can have some problems.

Many CMAs merely use from three to five comps to establish the average price per square foot. The square

Table 5.1 **Basic Competitive Market Analysis**

Features	Subject Property 8 Elm St.	Comp A 14 Oak Dr.	Comp B 36 Pine Ave.	Comp C 10 Elm St.
Price		$174,900	$189,900	$179,500
(Sales date)		(1/26/02)	(2/8/02)	(2/4/02)
Bedrooms	4	4	5	4
Baths	3.5	2	3	2
Square feet	2,658	1,936	2,550	2,555
Formal dining	Yes	No	Yes	Yes
Swimming pool	No	Yes	Yes	No
Age	1995	1999	1992	1996
Neighborhood		Superior	Inferior	Same
Price per square foot		$90.34/sq. ft.	$74.47/sq. ft.	$70.25/sq. ft.

Average price per square foot: $78.35

Indicated market value of subject property: $208,254

footage of the house being purchased ("subject property") is then multiplied by this factor to establish the listing price. Let's take a look at a basic CMA prepared by a listing broker.

In table 5.1, the price per square foot, $78.35, is based on the average of the three comps ($90.34 + $74.47 + $70.25 divided by 3). Using this method, the indicated value of the subject property is $208,254 ($78.35/sq. ft. × 2,658 sq. ft.). The CMA usually also provides an average selling price of the comps. This would be $181,433. However, in this case, the listing broker does not want to spotlight the average sales price because the subject property is the largest and best house in the neighborhood.

The next example of a CMA (table 5.2) shows why using the square foot method can give an inflated price. Here the agent makes some crude adjustments for major differences between the comps and the subject property, similar to what an appraiser does for the sales comparison approach of the appraisal process. The comps are adjusted to account

Table 5.2 **Better Competitive Market Analysis**

Features	Subject Property 8 Elm St.	Comp A 14 Oak Dr.	Comp B 36 Pine Ave.	Comp C 10 Elm St.
Price		$174,900	$189,900	$179,500
(Sales date)		(1/26/02)	(2/8/02)	(2/4/02)
Bedrooms	4	4	5 (−5,000)	4
Baths	3.5	2 (+6,000)	3 (+3,000)	2 (+6,000)
Square feet	2,658	1,936 (+36,100)	2,550 (+5,400)	2,555 (+5,150)
Formal dining	Yes	No (+3,000)	Yes	Yes
Swimming pool	No	Yes (−15,000)	Yes (−15,000)	No
Age	1995	1999 (−2,904)	1992 (+4,590)	1996
Neighborhood		Superior (−10,000)	Inferior (+10,000)	Same
Adjusted price		192,096	192,890	190,650
Indicated market value of subject property: $191,878, say $192,000				

for their differences with the subject property, with the adjustments listed in parentheses. The adjustments are based on the agent's experience of what people in the market will pay for various features. For example, consider the $15,000 adjustment for the swimming pool. In some markets, the swimming pool merits only a $5,000 adjustments. For markets in the north, a swimming pool adds no value due to the burden of winterizing the swimming pool when it cannot be used. Your agent should know which adjustments need to be made and for how much.

As you can see, by adjusting for differences, the more correct value is about $16,000 lower than the value suggested in the more basic CMA.

One reason the subject property value is lower than that listed in the first CMA is because it's the biggest and best house in the neighborhood. For that particular neighborhood, the house exceeds the market standard and will suffer a price discount. Many real estate experts warn buyers not to purchase the best house in the neighborhood. However, better advice is this: Don't pay too much for the best house. Negotiate to reduce the price to more realistic market standards. For the purpose of your negotiation strategy, you need to select a maximum market value for the property. Your CMA indicates $192,000. Notice however, that Comp C is right next door to the subject property. It also has the fewest adjustments. For these reasons, a better maximum target price might be $190,500. Before you establish your initial offering price, you need to consider other issues as well.

> ## Helpful Hint
> Don't rely on the listing agent's CMA to establish market value! *Remember:* The agent's commission is based on how much he or she can sell the house for.

Seller Motivation and Needs Analysis

A key factor in establishing a successful negotiation strategy is to judge the seller's motivation for selling the house. Or in other words, why is the house for sale? Motivations affect the seller's bargaining power. Some sellers can hold out for their target price. Others just want to get rid of the property as quickly as possible and are willing to lower their price and/or make other concessions.

How do you get the information? If you are dealing directly with the seller, you can just ask. He will probably tell you. If you take time to meet your future new neighbors, they may volunteer valuable information about the seller, the house, and the neighborhood. However, if you are dealing through the seller's agent, ethically she is not allowed to tell you if the information may be detrimental. Try telling the agent that you need to know so you can make an offer that meets the seller's real needs. Your buyer's agent can also check around or even be told inadvertently by the listing agent. Remember that your agent has a duty to tell you anything she finds out that can affect your judgment. The listing agent does not have this duty to you. Her duty is to the seller.

Let's look at how motivation can affect a seller's bargaining position.

Strong Bargaining Position

Is the seller being relocated, and has his corporation provided him with a guaranteed buyout price? This makes it difficult to get a significantly reduced price. However, some of these buyout plans only guarantee the seller his original purchase price, so find out how much he paid for it. Is the seller a retired couple planning to move to Florida or Hawaii? This couple doesn't need to move and probably won't sell unless they get a high enough price. If the seller occupies the house and you have no evidence that the current occupants have any need to move quickly (look for packing activities), the seller may not be under any real time pressure. If the house is being rented, the seller may actually be making money, which reduces any financial pressure on the seller.

Weak Bargaining Position

Has the seller lost his job, is he getting a divorce, or does he have health or financial problems? Problems such as these motivate the seller to make a quick sale and at a lower price. How long has the home been on the market? If it hasn't sold after more than ninety days, the seller may be willing to consider a lower price. Has the seller already bought another house on which he has to make mortgage payments? Is the house vacant? Is the seller under any time pressures? Does he need money quickly? Does he have to move quickly? What are the seller's monthly carrying costs (mortgage, property tax, insurance, and operating expenses)? Knowing how much the seller is paying each month can indicate a likely willingness to sell. If monthly outflows are high, this will apply more pressure to sell quickly.

What Are the Seller's Real Needs?

The price that the seller paid for the house is very useful information. You also need to know if the seller paid to make significant improvements. This will help you determine how much the seller will make from the sale. A second factor is to learn the existing mortgage balance on the house. Knowing this and the share of the seller's transactions costs (real estate commission and some other expenses), you can estimate how much the seller will net. Sellers will resist taking a loss. This information provides some indication on how far you can press on the price and other concessions. It is sometimes possible to increase the seller's net while reducing the price at the same time. For example, the buyer can agree to pay for some of the closing costs that are normally the seller's obligation.

> ### Helpful Hint
> Learn the seller's motivation in order to judge his bargaining power.

Determining How to Negotiate

Most people focus their negotiation strategy on the price. The listing price is the seller's initial offer to the market. What does the listing price reveal? How well priced is the listing? If the listing is within the ballpark of your CMA value, the seller is a serious player and is ready to deal. If the listing is high, the seller may just be testing the market and may not yet be in the game. If the listing price is low, move quickly—the seller may not know his property is underpriced. Or there may be serious defects with the house.

The Initial Offering Price

You can always increase your offer; however, lowering it is difficult. Therefore, make sure your initial offer isn't too high. For a listed price that is similar to your own CMA, consider making an offer 5% below the asking price. The seller expects this. If you offer the full price in a normal market, the seller will think either that you're stupid or that his listing price is too low. On the other hand, if the listing price is too high, consider a lowball offer. The seller may be a game player who wants a lot of bargaining room, and his strategy may be to try to meet buyers halfway. Making a low offer will frustrate that strategy. Your agent may warn you that this could insult the seller. If the seller is not yet

> If you offer the full price in a normal market, the seller will think either that you're stupid or that his listing price is too low.

ready to sell and the listing price is low, try making an offer close to the listing price. However, be sure it is subject to a satisfactory inspection.

When selecting your initial offering price, you also need to determine the maximum amount you are willing to pay. Keep this top price to yourself. *Do not* share it with anyone—not even your agent. To calculate the top price, imagine yourself trying to sell the house in five or ten years. How much do you think other people would be willing to pay for it? Smart real estate investors know that you make your money when you buy the house, not when you sell. Keep this in mind as you set your "walk-away price." In other words, if you can't buy the house for your maximum price, you have to be willing to walk away.

The Earnest Money Deposit

How much should you put down as an earnest money deposit with your offer? *Remember:* This money could be lost if you can't meet your end of the contract. Ensure that your contract is very specific as to what constitutes a default, as well as your right to have the deposit returned. It is generally recommended that you put down from 1% to 3%. If you are making an aggressively low offer, you may want to sweeten it with a much higher deposit.

Never make the check out directly to the seller or even the listing broker. Instead, make it out to the agent's trust account or to escrow. There are usually local regulations or practices that specify the best method. Don't forget that one of the most common consumer complaints to regulators is agents' mishandling of trust money.

Getting Ready to Bargain

You can prepare yourself for maximum power in negotiating a deal for a house in a number of ways. First, control your emotions. Analyze the potential purchase with your head instead of your heart. Know how much you can afford as well as how much you are willing to pay. There is a difference. You can only afford a set amount. However, depending on the house, you may set a maximum less than what you can afford.

Consider whether you should meet the seller face-to-face or work through your agent. This depends on your personal skills and on how much you can trust your agent. Make sure you are ready to deal and take care of anything that could cause problems during the negotiation. For example, get pre-approved for a loan so you can make a cash offer. Sell your existing house or arrange for the early termination of your lease so that you can close quickly. Prepare a well-thought-out contract offer and know what you are willing to trade off. In additions to these steps, you should also become familiar with the standard form contracts used in the local market.

Standard Forms

In most real estate markets, real estate brokers are used to dealing with one or more standard form contracts. Many versions of these standard forms may exist, depending on the location. Although some forms are preprinted, others are in software form and not printed until all information has been entered. Some states require the use of a state-approved or mandated form for all residential sales. Ask your agent for a copy of the forms everyone uses. Be sure you read each line in the contracts carefully and highlight anything you don't understand. Then ask your agent to explain these items to your satisfaction.

Agents actively encourage the use of these standard forms. First, they are familiar with these forms and may even have taken continuing education courses on understanding and filling out the forms. They know and trust these contracts. Second, although most states allow real estate agents to mechanically fill in the blanks of standard form contracts, the agent cannot draft original contractual language nor give you legal advice. For these things, you will need a lawyer. Third, and most important, much of the language in the standard form is written to protect the broker's right to a commission, reduce her legal liability, and limit the buyer's remedies against the broker. In other words, standard forms are there to protect the real estate brokers—not necessarily you.

> Delete any clause in the contract restricting you to mediation and binding arbitration.

Just because you use a standard form doesn't mean you can't change it. You may want to delete or change some of the language. For example:

1. Specify customary closing costs paid by buyers and sellers. Just because the contract or the agent states that "it is customary for the buyer to pay . . . ," doesn't mean you can't negotiate for something different. You may want to shift some costs to the seller as a concession instead of, or in addition to, lowering the price.

2. Delete any clause restricting you to mediation and binding arbitration. You want to preserve your right to

go to court if there is a serious dispute. You always have the option to agree to mediation or arbitration later.

3. Include other language your lawyer recommends. Although an agent is primarily concerned about her commission, you should be able to trust your lawyer to look out for you. She charges the same fee no matter what you pay for the house.

Standard form contracts used by homebuilders are particularly dangerous. Many of these are very one-sided. For example, if you buy a home based on a model and/or a set of plans, the builder does not guarantee when it will be finished. The builder also reserves the right to change elements of the house without notification and without your approval. Some contracts even allow the builder to switch your house to a different lot than the one you selected. If you want to make any modifications, you must agree to a "change order" that can substantially increase the price over what you originally agreed to pay. Finally, many builder contracts fail to include language making the contract valid only if you are able to obtain financing or other protections. You can be sure, however, that the contract includes language specifying the damages or fees you will have to pay if you don't keep your part of the contract.

> Never sign the contract right there in the homebuilder's office.

Never sign the contract right there in the homebuilder's office. Instead, take a copy home with you. Both you and your spouse should read it together several times, highlighting anything you don't understand. Then take it to your lawyer. Have him clarify any questions you may have and read the contract to make sure you are sufficiently protected.

Specific Requirements and Concerns

Your lawyer can also include additional language in the contract to make sure your specific requirements are carried out and any concerns are covered. In addition to price, you may wish to negotiate other factors. For example, you may need the seller to make available second mortgage financing or pay most of the closing costs so you have enough cash to close the deal. You may need time to sell your existing house, or you may need to close early so that you can move in as soon as possible. You may want certain inspections or repairs. If you want some items in the house, such as the custom draperies or the pool table, make sure this is spelled out in the contract. Don't assume the seller will leave them, even if he told you he would.

You, your agent, and your lawyer need to create a list of negotiation issues and priorities. Be sure to estimate how much each of these priorities is worth so you can make tradeoffs during the negotiation. For example, if the drapes are worth $500, don't increase the price for the house by $2,000 just to get the drapes.

Your attorney usually protects you by drafting "contingencies." These are statements that require something to occur before you are bound by the contract. If the specified event—such as securing a mortgage loan—does not occur, the contract is automatically cancelled. Likewise, a contingency can state that if something does occur, you are freed of an obligation. While negotiating your contract, you might want to include these issues:

1. In states that do not have mandatory seller disclosures, ask the seller to provide a written disclosure of any defects he is aware of on the property. This is especially useful if the seller is offering the property "as is."

2. What happens if the appraisal comes in below the price negotiated so you cannot get financing? You may

want to include the option to have the seller lower the price or allow you to walk.

3. What inspections are needed, and what cutoff dates are necessary to be able to have these inspections made before closing?

4. Is the seller responsible for repairs, or will he provide a repair allowance or a reduction in the price?

5. Will the seller pay for a home warranty?

6. Be sure to retain the right for a walk-through within 24 hours of the closing.

7. Make sure that the contract includes a financing contingency that allows you to cancel and to get back all of your deposits, if you cannot get the exact type of financing you require. The language should specify amount, interest rate, points, and term of mortgage, or you may be forced to take out a loan you don't want.

8. Which closing costs will the seller pay or share the cost of?

9. Will the seller pay points or make any other contribution to the financing?

10. When will you get possession? Is it before or after closing? Similar issues might include tenants on the property who need to vacate or a seller who would like to stay in the house until he can move into another house.

11. What personal property is included or fixtures excluded? Language in the contract should make clear that the seller cannot replace the light fixtures or other items.

Get Those Numbers!

Make sure that the registration numbers of important appliances are included in the contract. Sellers have been known to switch appliances if the description is too general. For example, assume that the contract stated "the refrigerator is included." You had seen a new Whirlpool side-by-side, 25.4 cubic foot refrigerator (Model: GD5SHAXKQ) when you examined the house. After closing, however, in its place you found a rusty 7.2 cubic foot refrigerator that had been stored in the garage.

12. Specify the condition standards that the property must meet at settlement. In other words, what happens if a tree falls on the roof or the hot water heater breaks?

13. If you see junk in the attic or basement or trash such as abandoned cars in the yard, specify that this must be removed before closing.

14. Additional issues will depend on other needs and concerns you have—or on local issues such as the description of water rights (important in Western states with the "prior appropriation" doctrine) and oil or mineral rights (very important in states like Texas).

Offers and Counteroffers

The formal process of negotiating a contract normally begins when you or your agent present a written offer containing all the issues you want. (States that use binders require an extra step to complete the process.) It is usually best to have your agent present the offer. She will also explain the reason for the price and some of the positive features in the contract. It's always a good idea to provide a context for the offer. Supporting information such as market comparables, price trends, the home inspection report showing costs of repairs, and other types of information can help the seller understand your reasons. This reduces the likelihood that the seller becomes upset or angry at your offer. If given the contract cold, the seller may react emotionally, especially if the price seems very low.

Your offer should normally have a short time fuse. Giving the seller no more than 24 hours to respond, for example, helps prevent the seller from using your offer to start a bidding contest with other potential buyers. However, in some circumstances, a longer period is appropriate, such as when the seller is out of the country. Ask your agent for guidance.

> It is normal for your first offer to be rejected and a counteroffer presented.

It is normal for your first offer to be rejected and a counteroffer presented. When a counteroffer is made, your original offer is considered void and can no longer be accepted unless you revive it by making it a second time. You and your agent should examine the counteroffer and determine whether to accept or make another counteroffer. The next section discusses the tactics for this part of the negotiation.

Strategies and Tactics for Successful Negotiations

You can choose from several different styles of negotiating. The "competitive style" is designed to win at all costs. It may be appropriate if the seller is also using this approach. It can end in impasse because no one is willing to compromise. The most typical approach is the "compromising style." Each party begins at a reasonable position and tries to meet the other halfway. The "collaborative style" is one of the more sophisticated approaches. It tries to find a "win-

win" solution with maximum results for both parties. The proper style depends on the relative bargaining strength of the parties, perceptions, personal values, personalities, emotions, and market alternatives.

You must understand that while the negotiation focuses primarily on price, this is not the only motivation of the seller. The way you and your agent treat the seller can make a big difference. Keep in mind that the seller has lived in the home for many years and may have invested a lot of pride and emotion in the place. He also wants to be treated fairly. If the seller starts to believe that you or your agent are trying to take advantage of him or are treating him or his home with disrespect, the deal might fail.

It is important that you or your agent can explain the market basis for a counteroffer so the seller understands it is reasonable and not "an insult." If you play the game of bluff and demand, are too stubborn to make concessions, or threaten to walk away, you may end up walking away without a signed contract. The more fair and realistic your offer, the more likely you are to buy the home of your dreams.

Even after you've signed the contract, you should give consideration to keeping the seller happy. Problems may arise before closing that require the seller's cooperation or additional negotiation. Even after closing, you may need to call on the seller for information ("Where is the water cutoff? The bathroom is flooding!!!!").

Tactics for Dealing Directly with the Seller

1. Usually negotiations are more successful if managed through an intermediary like your agent. There are cases where you may want to negotiate directly. For example, you are negotiating with an FSBO who refuses to deal with agents, or your agent has failed in his negotiation strategy and you are trying to save the deal. Another reason is that you believe you are a persuasive salesperson.

2. Negotiate confidently, make eye contact, and watch for signals from body language. Be careful about your own body language. Relax.

3. Backing the seller into a corner will limit your options. Also, do not turn the negotiation into a competition or allow either of you to get emotional.

4. Go slowly. Listen more than you talk.

5. Don't always try to meet the seller halfway. Consider using the "nickel and dime" tactic. For every dime the seller concedes, you only concede a nickel. Note that it is difficult to carry a negotiation past two or three rounds of offers and counteroffers. Trying to "wear down" the seller may only make him mad or more stubborn. Just as you can walk away, if you make him angry, he can refuse to have anything more to do with you and refuse to sell at any price.

6. Have a specific reason for your concession. Instead of raising your price, consider offering a different concession like an earlier or later closing date or a higher down payment. Plan your concession on the basis of timing and value. Always try to get concessions when you give concessions.

7. What are the seller's needs, and can they be satisfied more cheaply than making price concessions? Try to transform the discussion from a dispute to joint problem solving.

8. Use the costs of repairs in your professional home inspection to gain concessions. Pointing to facts in a written report is more effective than voicing your personal opinion that there are defects in the house. Your un-

supported opinion risks insulting the seller who may still love his home.

9. Try silence. This sometimes causes the seller to make further concessions or disclose information that you can use to propose acceptable alternatives.

> Trying to "wear down" the seller may only make him mad or more stubborn. Just as you can walk away, if you make him angry, he can refuse to have anything more to do with you and refuse to sell at any price.

10. Don't let trivial concessions get in the way of making the final deal.

11. Be willing to walk away from the deal. But do so with courtesy. If the house doesn't sell within the next couple of weeks, you want to keep the option open to go back—possibly with a slightly different counteroffer.

Tactics for Dealing Through Your Agent

1. Make sure you know whom your agent represents. You have to be a lot more careful about what you tell a listing agent, another seller's agent, or a dual agent.

2. Never tell your agent your final position. Let your agent know that if she can't get the right price from the seller, you will seriously consider one of the other top two choices you previously identified. If your agent knows you have realistic alternatives, she will work harder to get your price. Remember, she has a lot of time invested in inspecting this house and finding additional information. She certainly doesn't want to do it all again.

3. Be aware of the "good guy, bad guy" tactic. Usually, the husband plays the unreasonable "bad guy," while the wife or the agent plays the friendly, charming "good guy." People often make concessions to the good guy so they don't have to deal with the bad guy. The agent can be effective in playing the "good guy" if the other side doesn't realize that the agent doesn't really represent them. Usually, buyers fall for this tactic, but it can work both ways.

4. Using your agent allows you to apply the "limited authority" tactic. The negotiator has limited authority. After she makes the best deal, she indicates that the deal has to be "approved" by the boss (you, your spouse, co-investor, principal, and so on). When she comes back, she says the boss insists on further concessions. This is the classic tactic that some car dealers use. You can also create the power of limited authority by including a provision in the contract that it is "subject to review and approval" by your attorney.

5. Some people like the "non-stop negotiation" tactic. Even after the contract is signed, the other party comes back for new concessions after discovering new information or threatens to cancel the deal.

6. Are you or the other side using the "auction" tactic? Sellers claim that other buyers are just waiting to present an offer or even that they have made an offer. Buyers indicated that they are equally interested in two or three other houses.

7. Is the seller planning the "ambush at closing" tactic? If the seller is a competitive-style negotiator and has used the non-stop negotiation tactic, don't be surprised if he tries to ambush you at the closing by demanding more money or he'll cancel the deal. Also,

don't be surprised if an unscrupulous lender tries ambushing you with previously undisclosed fees and costs. Both of these individuals will think twice when they discover your lawyer will accompany you to the closing. Ambushes are more difficult if the closing is done in escrow (see chapter 7).

Tactics When the Price Is Right

1. If the price is right and the market is hot, do the deal and only include absolutely essential contingencies (such as financing).

2. If the price is right and the market is hot, make a full-price offer.

3. If the price is right and there are other offers on the table, offer more than the listing price with a very short time fuse (such as "two hours").

4. If the price is right and other offers are on the table, offer to pay all of the closing costs for the financing.

Examples of Win-Win Solutions

1. Get the seller to pay the closing costs in exchange for raising the price of the house. This makes no difference to the net received by the seller but reduces the money you have to produce at closing. This has to be coordinated with the lender, who needs to know this before they order the appraisal.

2. You and the seller have already agreed that the seller, an elderly couple, will pay for the repairs. However, the couple is unhappy about this. They really don't want to be bothered with the extra trouble of finding repairmen and contractors. Consider making a concession to

take the property "as is" and become financially responsible for the repairs in return for a price reduction. If you are a handyman, you might be able to make the repairs yourself rather inexpensively. However, if you haven't already paid for a professional home inspection, make sure you retain the right to cancel the deal if an inspection reveals serious problems.

Signing the Final Contract

Before you sign the final contract, read it carefully to make sure that it includes all agreements. Ensure that all blanks are filled out or have "N/A" or "not applicable." Check to see if all handwritten changes are initialed. Make sure all addenda are included and properly incorporated into the original contract. Check that all owners of the property have signed. If the sellers are married, it may be important for both to sign even if the title is only in one person's name. (Your lawyer can tell you why this may be important in community property and dower states.) Have the contract witnessed and notarized. Make sure both you and the seller have a signed original copy of the contract.

THE CONTRACT IS SIGNED—NOW WHAT?

In most markets, real estate transactions take 30–45 days to close after the final contract is signed. This time period can be longer because of requirements specified in contingencies, such as certain kinds of repairs or environmental inspections and tests. During this time, your agent will be working to resolve all contingencies and make sure that all necessary paperwork is processed in a timely fashion. Many service providers are involved in the process, including the title insurance company, the appraiser, the property insurance agent, and others. This stage is covered in chapter 7.

If you have negotiated and agreed to a signed contract, you have taken the sixth step. Congratulations!

6

Customizing
Your Mortgage

L et's go money shopping! In this chapter, we'll take a look at
the wide variety of mortgage loan programs. You'll also learn
about tools for custom designing your own mortgage loan.

So what is a mortgage loan? Also referred to as a "trust
deed" or "deed of trust" in some states like California, a
mortgage is technically not a loan. Instead, it is a pledge of
property to a lender in order to create collateral for a loan.
By signing a mortgage, you, the borrower, are the mort-
gagor. You are pledging your property to the lender—the
mortgagee. When borrowing money for a house, you receive
a mortgage loan—called a mortgage for short.

When designing your own loan, you need to make certain
basic decisions that are covered in this chapter. For example, you must decide:

Will you get a conventional mortgage loan, or do you
   qualify for an FHA (Federal Housing Administration)
   or a VA (Veterans Affairs) mortgage loan?

Will you make a down payment of at least 20%, or are
   you prepared to pay a monthly premium for mortgage
   insurance ("PMI")?

Will you get a fixed rate or an adjustable rate mortgage loan ("ARM")?

Will you get a 30-year mortgage term or a 15-year mortgage term?

Do you want to pay off your loan early by agreeing to bi-weekly payments instead of monthly payments?

Mortgage terms and options can be very confusing. Unless you understand what information to ask for and are able to judge advantages and disadvantages, you will probably not get the best loan. Consider the following example:

> Lancelot and Guinivere meet with a mortgage broker, Mr. Mordred, who offers them a choice of mortgage products. The first is a 30-year mortgage at 7.75% plus 2 points; it has a 5% down payment and a PMI of .78%. If they put 25% down, Mordred can give them terms of 7.5% plus 1 point. An ARM is available with a 5% annual teaser rate for the first year. It is tied to an index based on the "11th District COFI" plus a margin of 3%. It has an annual cap of 2% and a lifetime cap of 6%. Also available is the 3/2 Option of Fannie Mae's Community Home Buyer's Program.
>
> Smiling, Mordred asks: "Which mortgage would you like?"
>
> Shaking their heads, the couple leaves, knowing that they need to read this chapter.

 ## THE CREDIT QUARTET

You have two financial resources for determining the type of mortgage loan you'll be able to obtain. They are:

- **Down payment** (based on your savings and the gifts you can receive from friends or relatives)
- **Monthly payments** (based on the maximum permitted by the qualifying ratios)

The lender uses both of these to create hundreds of different kinds of possible loans using four factors known as the "credit quartet." The four factors are:

- Loan to value ratio (LTV)
- Interest rate
- Term
- Amortization (a big word but a simple idea)

Figure 6.1

TOOLS TO CUSTOM DESIGN YOUR MORTGAGE

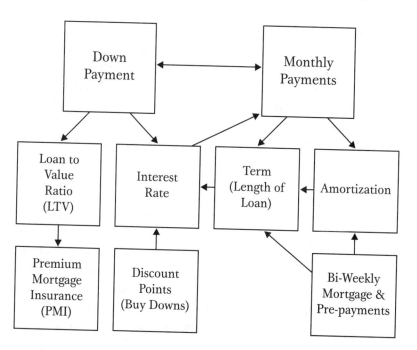

Figure 6.1 illustrates how these tools affect each other. For example, a high down payment will lower your loan to value ratio. A lower loan to value ratio (LTV) reduces the cost of the premium for mortgage insurance (PMI). If your LTV is below 80%, you may not need a PMI, depending on the type of loan. In addition, a higher down payment usually reduces the interest rate charged. These are also reduced by the payment of discount points or buy-downs. Decreasing the term (length) of the loan further lowers interest rates. Lower interest rates reduce the amount of the monthly payments. The size of your monthly payments can increase or decrease the amount of amortization (how quickly you pay off the loan). Changing to a biweekly mortgage and making pre-payments will both speed up the amortization and reduce the remaining term of the loan. Understanding these tools can help you custom design your mortgage loan. Let's look at each of these four tools in greater detail.

Loan to Value Ratio (LTV)

When you buy a house, your down payment represents the equity you own in the house, while the mortgage loan represents the debt. The LTV is a percentage relationship between the initial amount of the loan and either the contract price of the house or the appraised value of the house (whichever is lower). In other words, the LTV is a comparison between the amount you still owe on the house and what the house is worth. Let's look at an example of how this works. A house is appraised at $200,000, and the lender is offering an 80% LTV loan. Therefore, the maximum amount of the loan is $160,000 ($200,000 × .80 = $160,000). Over time, your house may appreciate while your debt decreases with each monthly payment. As a result, your equity is increasing and your LTV is decreasing.

Generally, a lender will not allow a borrower an LTV greater than from 75% to 80% because the lender needs a "margin of safety" in case the house is foreclosed. Foreclosure sales usually fetch a lower price than the actual market value of a house.

> A higher down payment usually reduces the interest rate charged.

Most borrowers qualify for conventional mortgage financing. By putting at least 20% down, they are able to acquire a loan with lower interest rates and avoid the costs of Private Mortgage Insurance (PMI). However, with PMI you can get loans with LTVs as high as from 97% to 100%. Lenders are willing to do this with certain government-insured or guaranteed loans such as FHA or VA mortgages. Finally, if you finance the home purchase with a land contract (contract for deed), it's also possible to have a very high LTV.

Let's talk about the range of financing choices from all-cash deals to high LTV deals.

All-Cash Deals

Some people have sufficient money to pay all cash for a new home. They often have an edge when negotiating a purchase. All cash greatly reduces the paperwork and lowers many costs to both the buyer and seller. For this reason, all-cash buyers are often able to negotiate a reduction in the seller's asking price. They can also take advantage of opportunities where the seller needs a quick sale because of divorce, medical bills, unexpected unemployment, or other factors.

Those purchasing a property for all cash need to be extra careful and should seek the assistance of professionals such as real estate attorneys, home inspectors, their own appraisers, surveyors, and others. When a person buys a house and requires financing, the lender requires many safeguards to make sure the house is worth the price. They also want to be sure that the title is good, no taxes are unpaid, the house is not infested with termites, and other considerations are satisfactory to avoid disastrous consequences in the future. However, because an all-cash buyer does not go through a lender, these safeguards are not automatically available. Cash buyers must be careful!

Conventional Mortgages

Most people opt for conventional mortgage financing. Approximately 60% of the borrowers make a down payment of at least 20%. For conventional loans with less than a 20% down payment, you normally have to pay for PMI. A lender may choose from several companies for the PMI. The cost of this insurance is approximately from .4% to 1.5% of the loan balance (depending on the term of the mortgage) and is based on the amount of down payment you choose to make. PMI protects the lender from a default by the borrower. PMI does not protect the borrower even though it is the borrower who pays the non–tax-deductible premiums.

One example, taken from the Internet, shows how PMI differs based on the percent of the down payment and the type of loan. Each mortgage insurance company will have its own schedule based on local risks in its market.

Percent Down Payment	Premium for 30-Year Fixed Mortgage	Premium for 15-Year Fixed Mortgage	Premium 1-Year ARM Mortgage
5%	.78%	.72%	.92%
10%	.52%	.46%	.65%
15%	.32%	.26%	.37%

You will notice that the PMI payment is reduced when you increase the down payment. The payment is also reduced when the length of the mortgage is shortened from 30 years to 15 years. You can choose from a number of options for paying the PMI.

The first option, used by about 80% of all borrowers, is to pay on a monthly basis, with $\frac{1}{12}$ of the annual premium added to the monthly mortgage payment. At closing, usually at least two months worth of premium is impounded by the bank and placed in escrow.

The second option is called "single premium" mortgage insurance. This plan is available on loans with at least 10% down. Here you pay the entire premium up front, or it can be financed into the loan. This latter option can provide a tax deduction. (Or, in negotiations, you could ask the seller to pay for the single premium.)

Another option is for the lender to pay the premium and increase the interest rate. In this case, you would have no monthly PMI and your interest payment would be tax deductible. This is sometimes called "lender paid mortgage insurance" (or "MI"). If you plan to keep the property for less than seven years, this may make financial sense.

> The mortgage insurance payment is reduced when you increase the down payment or when the length of the mortgage is shortened from 30 years to 15 years.

The final option is called an "80-10-10" or a "piggyback" loan. Under this scheme, a borrower takes out a conventional 80% LTV loan as a first mortgage and a 10% loan at a higher rate as a second mortgage, then makes a down payment for the rest. Although this allows the buyer to avoid paying PMI, it is usually a bad choice. The high interest rate on the second mortgage usually wipes out any savings on the PMI, even considering that the interest on both mortgages is tax deductible. PMI on conventional loans is not permanent. Once your LTV falls to 80%, you can go to the lender and ask that the PMI be dropped. However, in the past, many lenders refused to do this and instead continued to collect the premiums for unnecessary or even non-existent insurance coverage. As a result, the U.S. Congress passed the Homeowners Protection Act. Effective for loans originating after July 29, 1999, lenders are now required to automatically cancel mortgage insurance after a home-owner pays down the mortgage to 78% of the original purchase price. However, you should still request it at 80% because this can save you several months or more of monthly PMI premiums.

FHA Insured Mortgages

The FHA (Federal Housing Administration), which is part of the Department of Housing and Urban Development (HUD), offers mortgages for single-family homes, residences with two to four units, and FHA-approved condominiums. You can get these mortgages for 15- and 30-year terms with a fixed rate, an adjustable rate, and buy-downs. The qualification ratios for FHA mortgages are 29% for principal, interest, taxes, and insurance (PITI) and up to 41% for PITI plus total monthly debt payments. As of this book's publication date, the maximum amount available through FHA mortgages for single-family homes ranged from $132,000 for low-cost communities to $284,810 for high-cost communities. Your lender can tell you what the FHA limit is in your area, or you can find the rate at the following Web site: wwwfhalibrary.com/. The LTV is based on the following schedule:

- 97% of first $25,000
- 95% of next $25,001–$125,000
- 90% of remaining balance over $125,000 up to maximum insured amount

So if you were buying a house for $125,000, your minimum down payment would be about $5,750 and your LTV would be 95.4%.

FHA mortgages are very good for first-time homebuyers. Nearly 70% of single-family FHA loans are made to this group. If you qualify, an FHA mortgage could be one of the better loans available to you. The FHA does not actually lend money; private lenders make the actual loans. However, the FHA insures the mortgage loans by charging a Mortgage Insurance Premium (MIP). This premium used to be very expensive, making them unattractive to many borrowers. However, in recent years the cost has dropped considerably. As of January 1, 2001, the initial cost of the MIP is 1.5% with a periodic rate of .5%. The annual payments are cancelled once you have achieved 22% equity in the house.

The FHA lender will order an appraisal, known as a "conditional commitment." This appraisal will note all required repair work that must be completed and reinspected prior to the close of escrow (this means prior to the title being transferred to you by the seller). FHA loans require termite inspections within six months of closing. Although the FHA does not guarantee that the home is free of defects, it makes every effort possible to have the property properly inspected and repaired before the FHA insurance is issued.

Nearly 70% of single-family FHA loans are made to first-time homebuyers.

VA Guaranty Mortgages

For eligible borrowers, VA (Veterans Affairs) guarantee mortgages are one of the best deals around. Unlike FHA, which is an insurance program funded by MIP paid by the borrower, VA is a guaranty program that is provided by the U.S. government at no cost to the borrower. Furthermore, you are not required to make a down payment, your closing costs are limited, the seller (or anyone other than the borrower) must pay the discount points, and qualification is easier than other kinds of mortgages.

The amount of the VA guaranty is called the entitlement. The entitlement at the end of year 2001 was $50,750 to veterans purchasing or constructing homes to be financed with a loan of more than $144,000. The amount of the guaranty is on a sliding scale, dependent on the amount of the loan.

Do You Qualify for a VA Mortgage?

In order to qualify, the borrower must be a member of the military, a reservist, a veteran, or an un-remarried surviving spouse. Eligibility also depends on how much time you served during different periods after 1940. Less time is required if you served during a war period than between or after war periods. You should check with the VA Regional Office if you have questions about your eligibility. To prove your entitlement, you must have a "Certificate of Eligibility" (Form 26-8320).

Because the guaranty is for the top portion of the loan, most lenders treat it much like a down payment. Although the VA does not set a maximum loan amount, for all practical purposes, lenders limit the loan to $203,000. This is the maximum amount of a loan that can be sold by lenders to the secondary mortgage market.

Although you do not have to make a down payment, you do have to pay a funding fee at closing, which is based on the amount of your down payment. For veterans, it's 2% for down payments less than 5%. It drops to 1.25% for down payments of 10%.

The maximum amount of the loan is based on the Certificate of Reasonable Value (CRV). This is a VA appraisal. Unlike the FHA process, the VA appraiser does not ordinarily conduct an extensive inspection. Therefore, you need to make sure that the property is checked for defects. However, buyers of new homes have some protection. Builders must give a one-year warranty that the home complies with VA-approved plans and specifications. For homes completed under VA or HUD inspection, the buyer may seek compensation for some structural defects if a request is made within four years of the original VA loan guaranty.

A Web site with current information on VA loans is www.homeloans.va.gov/.

Zero-Down Mortgages

Zero-down mortgages have higher interest rates, usually 1% higher than loans with 20% down payments. PMI is also higher. There is even a loan where the lender will let you borrow 103% of the sales price. Such a loan is risky, expensive, . . . and available.

Land Contracts

Land contracts are called various names in different parts of the country: "contract for deed," "land sales contract," "land contract of sale," "conditional sales contract," "installment land contract," and "agreement of sale." I prefer to call it a "BAD contract." This type of contract is a form of seller financing that can result in the equivalent of a 100% LTV.

Unlike a regular sales transaction, you don't get a deed until you've paid the money due, or a large percentage of the money due, for the property purchase. A land contract is available, in many cases, without a credit check or any closing costs. Some unscrupulous sellers prefer those who have bad credit because they want you to default after having made high monthly payments for many years. In its worst form, if you miss a single payment, the seller can treat all of your previous payments (even after many years of on-time payments) as *rent*. He can then proceed to *evict* you like any other deadbeat tenant. You rarely have the protection afforded a person who is in default of a mortgage. Usually, the monthly payments are considerably higher than typical rent payments; however, you get nothing back if you miss a single payment. It may also be difficult to take a tax deduction on your monthly "rent" payments.

With a good real estate lawyer and tax accountant on your side, you may be able to draft a land contract that provides some protection. Furthermore, your lawyer will probably arrange for your contract to be recorded in the public title records, which may allow you to avoid a worst-case scenario. Normally, you should consider a land contract as a last resort—only if no other financing is available.

> You should consider a land contract as a last resort—only if no other financing is available.

Lease-Options and Lease-Purchases

Lease-options and lease-purchases (rent to own) are similar to land contracts and combine rental, sales, and finance techniques. These allow the buyer to accept a lease for a set term (typically for 12 or 24 months), followed by an option to buy the property at a previously agreed price. A lease-purchase differs from a lease-option in that it requires you to purchase the property at the end of a set period. With a lease-option, you have a right to purchase the property but are not required to do so.

An advantage of these techniques is that you can acquire control and possession of a home with a small down payment or even none at all. Normally, the seller, who is still the owner, is responsible for paying the property taxes and insurance during the lease period and is usually responsible for paying to keep the property repaired. While the property hopefully appreciates in value, your purchase price is locked in. You may not have to meet any credit or qualifications tests. You may even be able to negotiate that all or a substantial portion of the "rent" will be applied to the down payment while you shop around for the best available financing. With this option, you get to "test-drive" the house and find any problems and defects, as well as its positives.

The advantage to the seller is that the price is likely to be higher than what could be achieved with normal financing. Because the property is a rental property, certain tax advantages exist, such as deductions for depreciation and operating expenses that normally would not be available to a regular homeowner. The rent charged is also likely to be higher than the market rent.

The person who will not be thrilled with a lease-option deal is your real estate agent. Normally, she will not be paid a commission until you actually exercise the option and buy the property. It's possible your agent may be owed a commission as soon as you begin the lease-purchase transaction. To prevent this, put a condition in the purchase agreement that the commission will be paid only from the proceeds at closing. Although your agent will resist the insertion of this language, remember that it's *your* money. Do what is in your best interest and don't worry too much about the convenience of either your agent or the seller's agent.

One danger with this technique is that the seller may not be able to deliver clear title when you finally close the deal. You can reduce this risk by obtaining title insurance. However, because the seller retains title, as evidenced by the public record, you can do little to stop him from taking out a new mortgage or placing other encumbrances on the property. Even if the seller is honest, someone might obtain a judgment as a result of winning a lawsuit and place a lien on the property.

You could have your lawyer record an option memorandum indicating that the property is under contract to be sold. However, the lender holding the existing mortgage on the property could exercise its rights under a "due on sale clause." Also, if the seller has to file for bankruptcy while you still haven't exercised your lease-purchase contract, the bankruptcy trustee could cancel it, leaving you with no legal rights to the property. Another problem could occur if the seller dies. Although you have contractual rights to the property, these might be tied up for years while the deceased seller's estate goes through probate.

Special Low Down Payment Programs

Fannie Mae has established its "Community Home Buyer's Program" for borrowers whose household income is not more than 100% of the local average area income. This flexible program has fewer restrictive qualifying guidelines. Products available include:

HomeStyle Mortgage—Allows the borrower to get a loan for the cost of the purchase as well as the renovation. The loan is based on the value of the house after renovation.

3/2 Option—Allows the borrower to get a loan with only a 5% down payment, with 3% coming from the borrower's funds and 2% coming as a gift from a relative, a nonprofit organization, or local government program.

Fannie 97—Allows the borrower to get a loan with only a 3% down payment.

Interest Rate

Most loans break down into variations of fixed-rate interest loans and adjustable-rate (ARM) interest loans. Let's take a look at the opportunities, as well as the dangers, of these loans.

Fixed rate loans are predictable. You will know exactly how much you owe each month. In a low interest rate environment, fixed-rate loans are the choice of most intelligent people. You are an *absolute fool, idiot,* or *dummy* to commit yourself to an ARM in a low-interest-rate economy. On the other hand, an ARM is not a bad idea if interest rates are high. Consider the following implications of each alternative.

Fixed-Rate Mortgages

At one time, fixed-rate mortgages were almost the only kind available. When interest rates are relatively low (below 8%

Loan Shopping—Online

The Internet makes it easy to shop around for the loan that's right for you. Do a search for home loans or mortgage loans and you'll easily find a thousand different sites. Some are advertised on television or radio and can be owned by a single lending company. At these sites, you can play around with a mortgage calculator to see what you qualify for. Try entering different down payments and monthly payments, with different interest rates and terms, to see how each affects one another. You can also use these calculators to see how much you can afford to borrow. You can even request a quote.

LendingTree (lendingtree.com) is a good site to visit when you're looking for a mortgage loan. It offers calculators and checklists to help you figure out what you need to do. A nice feature is the tool that enables you to get quotes for a loan. After filling out six pages of information about yourself and the home, you submit the information. LendingTree then gets you four quotes from different companies. These quotes can give you a good idea of the types of loans for which you qualify. Even if you don't go with these quotes, you can use them for comparison shopping.

to 10%), these are usually the best programs for most borrowers. The monthly payments are predictable, and there's no unexpected payment shock by sudden increases in rates.

Adjustable-Rate Mortgages (ARM)

The adjustable-rate mortgage was designed by lenders to shift the risk of inflation from themselves to unsuspecting borrowers. These loans can be very tricky. If you don't ask the right questions, you may regret it. Ask what the worst-case scenario is and what the maximum amount is that you'll have to pay. Sometimes borrowers who get ARMs suffer from "payment shock" after a couple of years when the monthly payment is drastically adjusted upwards.

The ARM has a variable interest rate tied to a financial index that rises and falls. The initial rate is usually lower than fixed-rate mortgages. However, later in the program, the rate is likely to exceed the fixed rate if the economy is inflationary. You can use literally dozens of indexes. Some of the more common ones are tied to U.S. government securities or to the costs of funds rates, such as a Certificate of Deposit (CD) Index, a Cost of Funds Index (COFI) for the 11th Federal Home Loan Bank District, the London Interbank Offered Rate (LIBOR), and others.

On top of the index, the lender adds a "margin" of 2% to 3%. Together these form the note rate or the actual interest rate charged to the borrower. One misleading feature is that ARMs are often advertised with "teaser" or "come-on" rates—very low, below market rates. However, the low rate typically lasts for a very short time, in some cases for only one payment, before the lender "adjusts" it to the permanent note rate. One useful feature that you need to understand is the cap. There is an "annual" cap and a "lifetime" cap. The annual cap, which indicates how much up or down the rate can adjust, is usually from 1½% to 2% in either direction. The lifetime cap, which is the maximum amount the rate can ever change over the life of the mortgage, is typically from 5% to 6%. *Important note:* The cap is tied to the note rate, not the teaser rate. Another consideration is how often the adjustment takes place. It could occur monthly, quarterly, semi-annually, annually, or over longer time periods.

> One nice thing about interest payments is that they are tax-deductible.

Another problem: What happens when there is a "gap" between what you are required to pay (as a result of the cap) and the market rate? Some programs make you responsible for the gap and add this amount back to your principal. This would result in your loan amount increasing from negative amortization.

Some programs have a conversion feature that gives you an option to convert to a fixed mortgage at some point in the term. For example, consider the two-step mortgage. This is an ARM that adjusts only once, either in five or seven years. After the one-time adjustment, it behaves just like a fixed-rate mortgage for the rest of the term.

Discount Points

Points are a form of interest prepaid to the lender. One point is 1% of the loan amount. Each point can reduce the interest rate by ⅛ to ⅛ of 1%. The borrower pays points, or if agreed to in the real estate agreement, the seller may pay the points. This lowers your monthly payments. However, in order to make this worthwhile, you usually have to keep the house for a number of years so that your monthly savings offset the amount of money you had to pay up front.

Buy-Downs

One way interest rates can be lowered for the first year or two is through a buy-down. Builders often use buy-downs to reduce the initial monthly payments. This makes it easier for more people to qualify to buy the homes. This is also a concession you might be able to negotiate from the seller. Lenders allow individuals to reduce interest by pre-paying the difference between the buy-down rate and the market rate. For example, a 2-1 program means that the rate is reduced two percentage points during the first year and one percentage point during the second year.

Special Low-Interest Programs for New Homebuyers

States and local housing agencies offer programs for first-time buyers. These are funded by issuing tax-free bonds and are thereby able to offer below-market interest rates. Because first-time homebuyers must meet income guidelines, these programs are not for rich people. Many first-time homebuyers qualify for these programs. However, the house you want to buy must be priced within the limit of the program.

Term

The "term" refers to the length of time you have to pay back the mortgage loan. Longer terms mean lower monthly payments but more overall interest that you will pay to the lender. One nice thing about interest payments is that they are tax-deductible. Lenders consider longer terms to be more risky, so they charge slightly higher rates to account for the increased risk. On the other hand, because the monthly payments are lower for longer-term loans, you can qualify for a larger mortgage loan.

Let's take a look at a $100,000 loan with an 8% interest rate and see what happens to both the monthly interest and total interest when we vary the term in five-year increments. The most popular choices are 15-year and 30-year terms.

Term	Monthly Payment (8% annual rate)	Reduction from Previous Term	Total Interest Paid over Life of Loan
5 years	$2,027.70	N/A	$21,662
10 years	$1,213.30	$814.40	$45,596
15 years	$955.70	$257.60	$72,026
20 years	$836.50	$119.20	$100,760
25 years	$771.80	$64.70	$131,540
30 years	$733.80	$38.00	$164,168
35 years	$710.30	$23.50	$198,326
40 years	$695.30	$15.00	$233,744

You'll notice that something remarkable happens to the monthly payment as the term is extended. If you increase the term from 5 years to 10 years, the monthly payment drops a whopping $814.40 (from $2,027.70 to $1,213.30). But if you increase the term from 35 years to 40 years, the monthly payment drops only $15.00. Let's look at this in another way. Reducing your payment by $15.00 for the 40 years will reduce your cash outflow by $7,200 ($15.00/month × 48 months). However, for this privilege, you will pay an additional $35,418 in interest ($233,444 − $198,326). In other words, *just don't do it!* Do not take out a 40-year mortgage—you lose too much money. If you extend a 30-year term to 40 years, you'll reduce your monthly payments by only $38.50 per month at a cost of about $69,576 in extra interest paid.

Let's compare the two most popular terms—the 15-year and the 30-year mortgage loans. The 15-year mortgage loan costs you $955.70 per month compared to the $733.80 per month payment for the 30-year loan. This reduces your payments by $221.90 per month in cash payments. By extending it to 30 years, you will have to pay $92,142 in extra interest. Now you may think that the best loan is the one with the shorter term. However, this is not necessarily true. By taking a 30-year term, you can qualify for a larger loan. For example, if you could qualify for a $200,000 loan with a 15-year term, at the same interest rate, you could qualify for a $260,000 loan. That's a big difference.

Amortization

One of the most unpleasant facts about borrowing is that someday you'll have to pay the money back. But did you know that every time you make a mortgage payment, part of that payment is "amortization," a kind of savings program that makes you richer?

Amortization is simply paying back the principal you borrowed. There are five general types of amortization—accelerated amortization, full amortization, partial amortization, no amortization (interest only), and negative amortization.

Accelerated Amortization

Many lenders offer a special program called a "biweekly mortgage." Under this program, you pay half the monthly payment you would normally pay on a 30-year mortgage every two weeks. You would make twenty-six of these half-payments each year. In other words, this would create a full extra payment each year. Under this system, you could pay down your loan in about twenty-two years. If your budget can afford it, this is a good way to save tens of thousands of dollars. However, be sure to check with your lender. Some charge a set-up fee to do this or a surcharge on each payment.

> Many lenders offer a special program called a "biweekly mortgage." If your budget can afford it, this is a good way to save tens of thousands of dollars.

Another way to accelerate the amortization, and to avoid possible fees for biweekly payments, is to make periodic pre-payments. Make sure the lender allows you to do this without paying a pre-payment penalty. You also want to make sure the lender credits this to the principal. Some lenders put this payment first into the escrow account for insurance and taxes, and then any remaining money goes to interest. Although this is to their financial advantage to do it this way, it's not to your advantage.

Full Amortization

Most mortgage loans fully amortize over the term of the loan. Initially, most of each payment is interest, while only a small part is amortization. As the loan matures, more and more of each payment pays off the principal (amortizing the loan). For example, in a $100,000 loan at 8% interest over a 30-year term, your first monthly payment of $733.77 is $666.67 interest and $67.10 amortization. In the first year, you will have paid off (amortized) only $835.39 of your principal and paid tax-deductible interest of $7,969.85. After five years, your total amortization is less than 5% of the original loan. After ten years, you still owe $87,575.66, but now $585.82 is tax-deductible interest and $147.95 is amortization. After twenty years, you still owe $60,477.60, but now

$405.38 is tax-deductible interest and $328.39 is amortization. Positive amortization occurs only if the monthly payment is higher than the monthly cost of the interest.

Partial Amortization

This occurs when the monthly payment is more than the interest payment but less than the payment necessary for full amortization. This means that the loan will not be fully paid off at the end of the term. At the end of the term, you still owe money and will have to make a lump-sum payment for the principal still owed. This is called a balloon payment.

No Amortization

If your payments are exactly equal to the interest owed, you will have no amortization. At the end of the term, you will make a balloon payment equal to the original principal borrowed. In other words, each month you are only paying for the privilege of borrowing the money. The amount you owe remains the same.

Negative Amortization

If your payments are below the amount necessary to pay the interest owed, the portion of the unpaid interest is added to the principal. In other words, your debt grows as this happens. An example is the reverse annuity mortgage (RAM). While not available for new homebuyers, it is typically available to people who own their homes free and clear of any debt. A bank agrees to pay these borrowers a monthly payment that creates an increasing debt. The debt is then paid when the house is sold or when the borrower dies and insurance pays the debt.

A graduated payment mortgage (GPM) incorporates negative amortization features. This is a terrific program for young couples anticipating salary increases in the near future. These programs start with payments lower than level-payment mortgages. This means that the monthly payments do not cover all of the interest owed, with the difference added to the principal balance. After a series of steps over several years, the monthly payments are increased to fully amortize the new balance and are now higher than those for a level-payment mortgage. This program allows a borrower to qualify for a larger loan because the initial mortgage payments are lower. The GPM is also a good idea for a borrower who plans to move within five to seven years.

 # HOW DO LENDING LAWS HELP PROTECT YOU?

A number of federal laws provide protection for borrowers. Let's take a closer look at two of them and how you can benefit from them.

Truth in Lending Act

This disclosure law requires lenders to tell you the finance charge and the annual percentage rate (APR). The finance charge includes interest, origination fees, discount points, credit report fees, and other charges imposed to obtain the loan. The APR is the effective interest rate you are actually paying. It takes into account the points you must pay for the loan and allows you to compare different quoted rates.

Equal Credit Opportunity Act

This act prevents lenders from discriminating solely based on race, religion, national origin, color, gender, marital status, or age. Prior to this law, lenders used to charge higher fees for women and minority ethnic groups.

 # COSTS AND HIDDEN COSTS

When shopping for a mortgage loan, be sure to ask what fees you'll need to pay. These include application fees, title examination and title insurance, survey fees, document preparation fees, appraisal, lawyer fees, credit report fees, recording fees, escrow fees, notary fees, transfer taxes, PMI, and others. Some fees may be grouped together. Ask what services you are getting for the fees.

Watch our for junk fees! Always ask about fees *not* included on the good faith estimate. Try to get the lender to waive these, because they were not listed up front. You may have to talk to a manager, but doing so can be worth the time it takes. Do not accept services you don't need, such as credit life insurance. Some lenders are just like car rental companies; they will try to pack on fees for services you can refuse.

> ## Helpful Hint
> It's a good idea to review with the lender the list of fees in the mortgage agreement, asking what each is for and whether you really need to pay it. This may take time and seem like nit-picking, but it is your money.

Pre-Payment Penalties

Pre-payment penalties can be an unpleasant surprise if you were unaware of them. This is a fee that you are charged if you pre-pay your loan. This doesn't always apply to just pre-paying in full; it also can apply to partial pre-payments or paying a portion of the principal balance yearly. Before you accept the loan, check what the penalty is and negotiate to have it removed. Ask the following questions:

1. Is there a pre-payment penalty?
2. How is it calculated?
3. Does the penalty period end at a certain date?
4. Can I make extra payments to principal? If so, how much can I pre-pay each year?

Lock-Ins

If you believe that interest rates are going to increase, consider getting a "lock-in" in writing. These lock-ins require that the loan be closed with a specific time period. Ask the following questions:

1. Is there a cost to lock-in?
2. When does lock-in begin and when does it end?
3. If rates fall before closing, will you allow me the lower rates and lock those in?

Assuming a Loan

This topic involves two issues: First, can the loan you are taking out be assumed by a new borrower if you sell your home in the future? Second, can you assume or "take subject to" the mortgage of the seller? Prior to the 1980s, this was a popular option because restrictions on assumptions were few. Today, virtually all mortgage loans have "due on sale" clauses, which require the seller (original borrower) to repay the loan when the property is sold or placed under a long-term lease. Sometimes new buyers are permitted to assume the loan if they meet the bank's underwriting standards and pay certain fees. When you are allowed to make a mortgage assumption, you become personally responsible for making payments. Ordinarily, the original borrower is still secondarily liable and must make up any payments you fail to make unless the bank has agreed to substitute you as the person solely responsible for making payments. This substitution is called a "novation." If you "take subject to" a mortgage, you do not accept personal responsibility for the loan. So, if you default, the lender cannot sue you personally for a deficiency judgment. The original borrower remains primarily and personally responsible for the loan.

If you have customized your mortgage, you have taken the seventh step. Congratulations!

7

Closing and Moving In

You've signed your contract. You've been pre-approved for a loan. You've called the movers. You think the house is yours; all you're waiting for is the closing. You even start to choose your new furniture for the living room. Stop right there. Don't get ahead of yourself. Over 25% of buyers never complete the final step and close the transaction.

Many things can go wrong before closing—the title may be defective, the survey may reveal serious encroachments, the house may burn down, you may lose your job, you may be transferred, interest rates may skyrocket, scheduled repairs may be more expensive or impossible to make, or another unexpected event may occur. If you come unprepared to the closing, you may find unexpected fees that have been charged or documents that you have to sign that are incomprehensible. You may also encounter surprises after you have received title and moved into your house. Consider the following example:

> Ashley and Melanie did a final walk-through of Tara. They were satisfied with the extensive repairs and the remodeled kitchen. When they showed up later in the

day to close, they were given a pile of documents to sign. Among these were a mortgagee's title insurance policy and an assignment of lease. The escrow agent was impatient because she had three other closings scheduled that afternoon. They hurriedly signed and left the office. When they tried to move in, they discovered a tenant in possession named Scarlett O'Hara. She smiled sweetly and said she'd be happy to share the house until her lease expired in two years. Three months later they received a $125,000 bill for the remodeling. The subcontractor had not been paid and had filed a mechanic's lien. They then discovered that they had no title insurance to protect them. The mortgagees' policy only covered the lender.

PREPARING TO CLOSE

After you and the seller sign a contract, someone has to "open" escrow or notify a closing attorney that a closing needs to take place. This is usually taken care of by the lender or the agent of the seller—but not always. If you have dealt directly with the seller, either one of you can open closing. To do this, just give your "good faith" deposit to the escrow agent or closing attorney and provide him with all documents and any written instructions.

In order to close, you need to finalize your financing. For this your lender usually requires a number of reports, including a credit report, a preliminary title report, an appraisal, and a survey. He will also need a payment for a lender's title insurance policy as well as a fire and hazard insurance policy. During escrow, both your financing and closing must come together at the same time because each relies on the other for completion.

Find a Closing Agent

Lenders usually have a preferred closing agent. However, you are not required to use their agent. In fact, you may be

Shopping for a Closing Agent

The Internet is an easy way to shop around for a closing agent. If your state requires an attorney, check out the Martindale-Hubbell Lawyer Locator at www.martindale.com. However, if you can use an escrow company, hundreds are available. Go to a search engine and enter the name of the state in which you are purchasing and the word "escrow." For example, if you are purchasing in New York, type in "New York escrow." This will help narrow down your choices to companies that operate in the state. Also be sure to try Escrow and Title Service.com (www.escrowandtitle service.com). This site is a bit easier than using a search engine. You just choose the state and then select from the list of companies provided. The hyperlinks will take you right to the Web sites of these companies where you can get more information.

able to save money by shopping around for a different escrow agent or a closing attorney. Which one you will need depends on the requirements of your state.

What Does a Closing Agent Do?

Your attorney can provide written instructions for the escrow officer. In simple cases, the real estate agents, both the buyer's and the seller's, agree to standard form instructions. A file number is issued, and the closing process is set into motion. In non-escrow closings, the closing attorney provides similar services. The escrow agent serves as a neutral referee, holding all the money deposited and all the documents until it's time to distribute the money and transfer and record the documents. Then you get the good news that you now have the deed and own the property.

What Else Do You Need to Do?

You are also likely to have a number of contingencies and deadlines to complete before closing. Your buyer's agent will monitor and coordinate many of these activities for you. Make sure you know what she's doing and what you need to do. Create a punch list so that no major action is forgotten. Speaking of which . . . did you call the mover?

Don't forget to cancel utilities, newspaper delivery services, and other regular services at your old place and establish them at your new home. Be sure to notify the post office of your change of address. This should be done at least one month prior to the time you expect to move. You don't want to be hit with late charges by some of your creditors because you did not receive their bills on time.

Helpful Hint

If you're renting an apartment, you need to notify your landlord that you will not be renewing your lease. Give your notice in writing and include a specific day when you will be leaving. Hopefully, you made prior arrangements in anticipation of this move and changed to a month-to-month rental agreement or arranged for early termination of a fixed-term lease.

If you have small children, spend some time with them to help prepare them for the move. You may be stressed out about the move, but they are likely to be even more so, especially if this is their first move. Children don't like change. As you're preparing to move, watch for sudden changes in behavior or personality. It's also important to get them involved. Take them on a walk-through of the house. Let them know where their bedroom will be located. Let them take part in some of the planning, such as choosing wallpaper for their new room or deciding where their furniture will go. As long as you keep them informed and involved, children will be more comfortable with a move, especially if they benefit from a larger bedroom, a bedroom or their own, or a great backyard or pool.

KEEPING YOUR RECORDS ORGANIZED

In the days after the contract is signed, you'll begin to receive notifications and other information in the mail. You may also get verbal information from various parties, including the seller. It's important to keep this information together and organized or you may forget things you'll need at closing or afterwards. Some of this information will be needed later when you prepare your income taxes. You may also need some of it when communicating with your lender in the future. Go to your local office supply store and buy a plastic file box. Use dividers or folders to organize the information you receive before, during, and after closing. It's also a good idea to keep a journal of all verbal information that you're given. Include the name of the person, phone number, time and date, and what was said.

Paper, Paper, and More Paper

When you decide to buy a house, get ready to be overwhelmed by paper. Much of this is for your own protection. You'll receive several disclosures required by RESPA, which stands for the Real Estate Settlement Procedures Act.

The first information will usually arrive within three days of applying for a loan. The lender will provide the Truth in Lending Disclosure Statement and a Good Faith Estimate of Settlement Costs, which details the costs you must pay for your loan and the purchase of the house. Because some of the costs are not known at the time of your loan application, the

> When you decide to buy a house, get ready to be overwhelmed by paper.

lender provides a range of costs for the unknown items. Look over the Good Faith Estimate and make a list of questions about any fees you don't understand. Then get in touch with your lender and get answers to all your questions. Don't forget to ask if each fee is required. In the previous chapter, we discussed junk fees or unnecessary fees tacked on by some lenders that you can ask to be waived. You will also receive a HUD booklet titled "Settlement Costs and You." This booklet will guide you through the most complex document in the closing—the HUD-1 Settlement Statement—so take time to read it.

Expect to receive an "Appraisal Notice" from your lender. This will advise you of your right to a copy of the appraisal report for which you paid. However, the lender will not automatically give it to you; you must request the report in writing. Be sure to do so. It can be extremely helpful. For example, it's useful for establishing a depreciation deduction if you set up a home office in your house or if you rent a portion of or the entire house to tenants. You can also use it to determine how much fire and hazard insurance to buy or, if necessary, to appeal a high property tax assessment.

> **Helpful Hint**
>
> Keep any brochures advertising your house. You may be able to use these when you resell the house many years in the future.

Another informative document is the "Private Mortgage Insurance Disclosure." The disclosure advises you about the difference between traditional mortgage insurance (MI) and lender-paid mortgage insurance. Discuss this with your lender. Depending on how long you plan to stay in the house, one may be cheaper than the other. Generally, the less time you plan to live in the house, the more cost-effective the lender-paid mortgage insurance will be. This type is financed at a higher interest rate but is tax-deductible.

The lender may also provide you with a "Transfer of Servicing Disclosure Statement." This advises you that the lender may be planning to sell the servicing of your loan to another company. Another common form is the "Affiliated Business Arrangement Disclosure," which states that you do not have to use the providers recommended by the lender and are free to shop around for your own. At closing you'll get a copy of your promissory note, which specifies the dates your mortgage payments are due, and a copy of your mortgage or trust deed. Try to get copies of these before closing so that you and your lawyer can review them without being rushed. Pay particular attention to any pre-payment clauses, any interest escalation language, and any unusual default provisions.

After you have moved into your house, continue to collect and organize the additional records you receive. If you're purchasing a new home, be sure to keep all documents the builder gives to you. It is crucial to locate all manufacturers' warranty cards for appliances and systems such as air-conditioning and heating. Fill them out and send them in. The builder's sales representative may have provided some of these cards in a nice package. Others may be in kitchen drawers or attached to or even inside the appliances. Sometimes you receive these during your final walk-through. Before you test out the washer or the oven, look inside and remove the warranty and owner's manual. Keep a list of when the warranties expire.

WHAT'S IN A TITLE?

At closing, you'll get legal title when you receive the deed. Normally, you have the right of possession at midnight on closing day. Customs vary in certain areas. Ask your buyer's agent for the exact time you are entitled to possession. You and the seller can change this time by mutual agreement.

Holding the Title

Before closing, you need to determine how you are going to hold the title. This information is necessary to properly draft the deed. You can hold title in your own name (title in severalty), you can hold it with another person (tenancy in common), you can hold it with another person with rights of survivorship (joint tenancy), or you can hold it with a spouse (tenancy by the entirety). You can also choose to create a partnership, corporation, limited liability company, or trust to hold the property for you. Each of these alternatives has control, tax, inheritance, and other legal consequences. It's important to ask an attorney for guidance.

What Property Rights Are You Purchasing?

What property rights are you acquiring? Are you buying a "fee simple" or something less? The fee simple is the most ownership the law will recognize that individuals can have. If you are buying a home on leasehold land or a qualified fee (a property subject to conditions, which if broken, can terminate your property rights) or a property with easements, make sure you know what you are actually buying. In Western states, get advice on what water rights you have. For states like Texas, be sure you know whether you are getting the mineral or gas rights. If you are close to a river or a lake or the ocean, find out about your riparian and littoral rights. (Riparian rights refer to your right to use water in a stream or river passing through your land; littoral rights are to water in a bordering lake or ocean.)

Types of Deeds

Many kinds of deeds can be issued. These are classified in two broad categories—warranty deeds and quitclaim deeds.

The general warranty deed contains covenants (promises) in which the seller (grantor) guarantees good and marketable title to the buyer (grantee). This deed has the most promises. Specially warranty deeds, grants deeds, and bargain and sales deeds are less desirable. These do not have the same level of promises by the grantor.

Quitclaim deeds have no covenants. These give only whatever property rights are owned by the grantor at the time the deed is delivered. If the grantor has nothing, you get nothing. If the grantor has perfect title, you get perfect title. There are numbers of special purpose quitclaim deeds, including administrator deeds, executor deeds, guardian deeds, sheriff's deeds, deeds in foreclosure, tax deeds, and others.

Even if you receive a general warranty deed, this does not guarantee that you are being given good and marketable title. It's necessary to examine the chain of title in the public records to be assured that the grantor has good title to give. However, even examination of public records will not protect you from title defects known as "clouds on title." Examples of clouds on title include deeds issued without release of dower, forgeries, death of grantor prior to delivery of deed, missing heirs, clerical mistakes in indexing documents, mistakes in posting taxes, and different kinds of frauds or mistakes.

> ## Helpful Hint
>
> If you're planning to hold the property with a friend or a relative other than your spouse, you need additional legal counseling. For example, you'll probably need a written agreement to handle issues such as buyouts, share of maintenance and repairs, dispute resolutions, and other potential problems.

Title Assurance

For these reasons, most people don't rely solely on the deed. Instead, they seek some external review of the quality of title or title insurance. In some states, an attorney or a professional abstractor prepares an abstract of title. This is a summary of all deeds, mortgages, easements, and other documents in the chain of title. An attorney analyzes the abstract and issues an attorney's opinion of title. However, if the attorney makes a mistake, your only recourse is to sue. (*Consumer hint:* It is very expensive to sue attorneys. Suing is their business, and they are good at it. Try not to sue attorneys!)

A better approach is to take out title insurance. Title insurance is available in all states except Iowa, which has a

Preliminary Insurance Report

If you have decided or are required to have title insurance, you will first receive a preliminary title insurance report. This does not insure you until you have paid a one-time premium for the coverage and then only if you purchase an owner's policy. The lender or mortgagee will require you to purchase a policy to cover their interests. However, this policy offers you no protection, so make sure you're covered. Read the preliminary report and ask your attorney to review it. This will tell you what defects in title may exist and what is covered by the title insurance policy.

title guarantee program. Lenders almost always require title insurance. It's recommended that title be searched up to the day of closing. A few states also have title registration through a Torrens System. This is similar to the system used for automobile registration. The Torrens certificate has the name of the current owner of the property. When an owner dies, or a property is sold, a new certificate is issued.

The most common title insurance policy is referred as an ALTA title policy. This is based on guidelines specified by the American Land Title Association. ALTA has a separate policy for lenders (mortgages) and owners. Your lender will require that you buy the lender's policy. It only covers the lender from any title defect losses affecting the mortgage loan balance. After the loan is paid off, and the lender is out of the picture, this coverage disappears. The bad news is that the lender's policy does not cover the owner (buyer). The good news is if you buy the owner's policy at the same time as the lender's policy, you'll receive a substantial discount.

By paying a one-time premium, from approximately .4% to .7% of the purchase price, you are covered from title defects that occurred prior to your purchase of the property for up to the amount of the purchase price. Shop around to find the best rates and costs for title insurance. For example, if the seller has only owned the property for a short time, check to see if the title company will reissue the seller's title policy to save you money. If you want inflation protection, you can usually get this by paying an extra premium. The insurance policy also pays the costs of defending your title.

Basic coverage, contained in Schedule A of an ALTA title policy, includes twenty-nine specific types of protection, including title defects; easements; rights out of leases, contracts, or options; forgery or impersonation; prior mechanics liens; lack of access to property; loss of property due to prior violations of deeds restrictions; and violations of building permits.

ALTA also has a list of exceptions or exclusions in Schedule B. These are problems that are not covered and include such issues as construction liens, rights of Native Americans, and wetlands. If you are concerned about any of the exceptions, you can buy extended ALTA coverage for some of the standard exceptions.

Some states have standard title policies that are different from the ALTA policy. For example, California has the CLTA policy, while Texas has the ALTEX policy. These policies have different exceptions and exclusions than the standard ALTA policy. Be sure to consult with your lawyer about which type of policy to purchase and whether any of the exceptions could pose future problems.

SHOPPING FOR OTHER TYPES OF INSURANCE

All lenders require insurance for fire and hazard risks. They want to make sure they don't lose their collateral in your house. Depending on the area in which you will live, you may also be required to pay for national flood insurance or even earthquake insurance. A homeowner's warranty is very similar to insurance and protects you against defects or structural problems with the house. This may be provided by a builder or available from a third-party warranty company. Some real estate companies provide warranty programs to their seller clients. However, you should shop around for the best buy for each of these insurance products because those offered by agents are often more expensive than others you can find. Now let's look at some of the types of insurance you will need.

> All lenders require insurance for fire and hazard risks.

Homeowner's Property Insurance

At closing, most lenders require you to provide a one-year paid receipt for a homeowner's insurance policy. This is also referred to as a fire and hazard insurance policy. Be sure to shop around for the best rates and coverage or you may end up paying two or three times as much as you have to. Also, try to take advantage of discounts. To shop smart, follow these steps:

1. **Determine what kind of coverage you need.** You should worry about more than just damage to your own structure. What if someone slipped on your sidewalk? What if a tree branch from your property falls on your neighbor's roof? Homeowner policies come in five flavors. Additional policies are available for renters/cooperative owners (HO-4: Renter's Policy) and condominium owners (HO-6: Condominium Owner's Policy). Homeowner policies are either specific peril (HO-1: Basic Form; HO-2: Broad Form; HO-3: The Special Form; and HO-8: Older Homes Form) or comprehensive (HO-5: Comprehensive Form). The specific peril policies only cover you for losses speci-

fied in the contract. If you suffer a loss from something not listed, you are out of luck. For example, the Basic Form (HO-1) lists only eleven perils. Comprehensive is the best coverage and also the most expensive. It covers everything except losses from war, flood, earthquake, and other occurrences listed. You can get coverage for both flood and earthquake separately. These are discussed later in this section.

2. **Determine how much coverage you need.** Most insurance companies require you to carry coverage for at least 80% of the value of your building. If you carry less, you become a co-insurer of the loss. For example, suppose you are supposed to have $200,000 in coverage, but you are only carrying half of that ($100,000). What happens if you suffer a $50,000 loss? The insurance will only indemnify you for $25,000, even though you are carrying $100,000 worth of protection. Therefore, you want to be sure you are carrying at least the minimum required. Also, have your house value checked each year so you can adjust the insurance to the necessary amount. Consider adding "full replacement coverage"—otherwise, the insurance pays only for your depreciated loss instead of the actual cost to fix or repair the damage.

> At closing, most lenders require you to provide a one-year paid receipt for a homeowner's insurance policy.

3. **Shop around.** Get written estimates from at least three reputable insurance companies. Some state insurance commissioners provide consumer information and complaint ratios for companies licensed to sell insurance in their states. Use the Internet to get quotes as well as research the companies you are considering.

4. **Check for discounts.** If you buy from a company with whom you already have other types of insurance, such as car or renters insurance, you could get a discount of 5% to 15%. Members of an organization, such as a labor union, may qualify for an additional discount. Newer houses have discounts available as well. Some companies give additional discounts if you add a smoke detector, security alarm system, deadbolt locks, sprinkler system, and other safety features. One of the largest discounts is for increasing your deductible. For example, if you increase your deductible from $250 to $5,000, you could lower your premium by almost 40%.

5. **Make an inventory.** Keep an inventory of all your major purchases. Include information on purchase price (keep receipts) as well as where and when you purchased these items and their ID or serial numbers. Some insurance companies will provide inventory forms for you to fill out. Take photographs or videotape each of your major belongings. (If you have a digital camera, it's easy to store these images on your computer.) You may need a professional appraisal for valuable items like original art or antiques. By keeping all this information, you will be able to document your losses if you ever have to file a claim. This will not only speed up claims adjustments but also reduce disputes. Be sure to keep a copy of this list and your photos or videotape somewhere safe outside of the house—such as with a friend or relative or even in a safe deposit box.

Flood Insurance

Your home may be subject to flood risks even if it's not close to a river or lake. Melting snow, hurricanes, heavy rains, and backup of overloaded drainage systems can cause flooding. Flood damage is not covered under homeowner's policies. You can buy flood insurance that provides up to $250,000 worth of coverage for home and up to $60,000 for contents through the National Flood Insurance Program (NFIP). This carries a $500 deductible for the building and a separate $500 deductible for the contents. NFIP premiums are higher for homes with basements. If your home is in a low-risk flood zone (B, C, or X), you may be entitled to a discount under the Preferred Risk Policy (PRP).

Earthquake Insurance

An estimated 90% of the U.S. population lives in areas prone to earthquakes. Some states, such as California, Washington, and Missouri, are very prone to this danger. Areas are rated from 1 to 5 for likelihood of quakes, and the insurance premiums are based on this rating. Deductibles for earthquake insurance are high, and policies available through the California Earthquake Authority have a 15% deductible.

> Be sure to keep a copy of your inventory list and your photos or videotape somewhere safe outside of the house—such as with a friend or relative or even in a safe deposit box.

The Homeowner's Warranty

A homeowner's warranty is no substitute to having thoroughly inspected and re-inspected the house. It's only as good as the builder or third-party insurance companies that are willing to back it up. Before you buy a new house, check the reputation of the builder. If you buy a warranty on your own, call the state insurance commissioner's office and the Better Business Bureau to check the reputation of the warranty company. No matter what your warranty claims to cover, if the builder or insurance company that issued it doesn't stand behind the policy, it is worthless.

Warranties cover all workmanship and materials for the first year. Note that some states make the builder responsible for these repairs even without a written warranty policy. During the first two years, plumbing and electrical systems are usually covered. Major structural defects are usually covered for ten years in plans that last that long. The wording on insurance protection for major structural defects can often be tricky. For example, the warranty may not cover major structural defects unless these also affect the physical safety of the occupants of the house. Other problems, such as cracks, may have to be a certain width before they are covered, even though they may be unsightly. If you have made changes in the building, this may negate some of the warranty protection. Or if warranty repairs require the removal of some feature you've added, such as a tile floor, the warranty might not cover the cost of replacing any tile damaged during the repair. Likewise, any damage caused by your own neglect is not covered. For example, replacing carpet that has faded because of too much sunlight exposure is not covered.

> ### Helpful Hint
>
> Before you buy a policy on an older house, check to see whether the warranty even covers it. Houses usually have to meet current building code standards to qualify for coverage.

If you buy a homeowner's warranty, you can expect to pay from $350 to $500. In addition, each time you require a service call for warranty repairs, you can anticipate paying from $35 to $100 additional per call. Plans set a maximum amount that they will pay for repairs. You may also have to pay deductibles.

Third-party warranty companies usually require that you call repair people from an approved list. In some cases, the warranty company must order the repairs themselves. If you use unauthorized repair service people, the warranty company may refuse to reimburse your costs.

When considering a warranty, you want to have the following questions answered:

1. What does the warranty cover? What isn't covered? Usually, appliances and heating ventilation and air-

conditioning systems (HVAC) have their own warranties and are not covered under a homeowner's warranty. There usually is an extensive list of additional exclusions, such as damage from shifting soil, water intrusion, violation of building codes, and similar items.

2. What are the costs of service calls? Does the policy include deductibles or a cap on the amount that the warranty company will pay for repairs?

3. Ask the builder how his company handles warranty service. Does he have any referral letters from satisfied customers that you can see? If a state has a mandated new home warranty law, check with the warranty compliance office in the state insurance department for any complaints.

4. How quickly will the builder or warranty company respond to requests for repairs? How do they handle emergency repairs?

5. Does the warranty cover replacement and repairs or just repairs?

6. From what date do warranty protection periods begin? Is it when you sign the contract, close the transaction, move in, or at another point in time?

7. How are disputes resolved? Is mediation or binding arbitration required?

8. What is the financial stability of the home warranty company or the builder? Are these companies going to be around when you need them?

Make and maintain a punch list of items that require warranty work. Make sure that you submit your final list of required repairs to the builder before the first year's warranty protection period has expired. You might also consider having a professional home inspector look for items you may have missed. When you're seeking to have these repairs done, keep records of all verbal conversations and promises made to you. Write down in a separate file folder or on your computer times, dates, names of people you talked to, and what was said. When you are talking to the builder or his representative, always be polite but firm. Avoid getting angry or making threats. These tactics usually place your problems at the bottom of the builder's priority list.

If verbal requests are ignored, or if promises are not kept, consider the following approach: First, check to see whether the repair is covered by the warranty. Second, prepare a tactful letter describing the problem and the promises made. Include your record of past conversations and actions taken or not taken by the builder. Indicate what you want done and give the builder a reasonable time to complete the request. Third, follow up with a phone call confirming that your letter was received. If that doesn't work, consider filing a complaint with your state consumer protection agency or contacting your attorney. If the warranty requires mandatory arbitration, file a request for this process to be initiated.

GETTING READY TO CLOSE

As the time approaches to close the deal, you still need to do a few more things. Often you have only 24 hours, so make sure to schedule time for these tasks.

HUD-1 Settlement Statement (RESPA Uniform Settlement Statement)

RESPA requires lenders to provide you with the HUD-1 Settlement Statement one business day prior to closing. Do not waive this right. You must look this over very carefully and without interruption. You won't have this uninterrupted time at the closing. This is the final closing statement, which itemizes all the fees and charges that were credited or debited to your account. Make sure all the information is correct.

Compare the HUD-1 Statement to the Good Faith Estimate you received when you first applied for the loan. Question any major differences. For example, is the mortgage broker receiving a yield spread that was not previously disclosed? This is an extra fee paid to the broker for getting you to agree to an above-the-market interest rate. Are any costs included that you didn't expect? Some of these last-minute charges may be dropped if you inquire about them. Others may be legitimate and justified, but you are entitled to know why. Look for mistakes in your sales contract that may have some unusual addenda and modifications. The clerk preparing the closing documentation may not have noticed these differences and automatically charged various items the way they are customarily handled.

> **Helpful Hint**
> It's easier to resolve any problems with the closing statement before you close rather than later, after you have already agreed to pay the charges and they have your money. This is a good time for your buyer's agent to earn her money and resolve these problems.

Prorations will be different, and for a good reason. These are based on the day and month on which the closing takes place. Payments for mortgages are made in arrears. In other words, your payments for a certain month are made at the end of the month. For example, your mortgage payment for July is paid at the end of July. Therefore, at closing, the mortgage you pay for the first month is prorated based on the number of days you own the property during that month. However, no payment for the next full month is due until the last day of that month.

Keep the final closing statement for income tax reasons. Some of the items on the HUD-1 statement are tax-deductible. Other information may be needed for taxes in subsequent years.

THE FINAL WALK-THROUGH

Do not miss this step. Your contract should reserve for you the right to a final walk-through before closing. Do this carefully with your real estate agent. If you see something wrong, have your lawyer or agent resolve it before closing. Don't contact the seller directly. This could lead to an emotional clash.

The reason it's so important to resolve these problems before the closing is because of a common law doctrine called "merger." This specifies that once the deed is delivered and accepted, the original contract and its provisions disappear. For example, the seller may have agreed in writing in the contract to include household appliances as a part of the sale. However, when you do your walk-through, you see that all the appliances have been removed. If you close without first resolving the problem, you are agreeing to accept the house as is—without the appliances. Therefore, unless the provisions were drafted to "survive" closing, which is very rare, you must resolve all problems before closing. This may mean setting money aside in an escrow account until the dispute is settled or postponing the closing. At times like this, you will find your attorney invaluable.

THE CLOSING

The closing is the process of title being transferred from the seller to the buyer. It's called "closing," "settlement," "escrow," or something similar. Closing practices vary by state. In some states, you have a closing around the table where you, the seller, the lender, the two real estate agents, the closing attorney, and others meet together and pass documents and checks back and forth. In other states, you and your real estate agent sit alone with the escrow officer and sign the papers. The seller signs his papers separately as well. The escrow officer processes all the necessary paperwork and disburses the necessary funds. When this process is finished, you receive the deed and keys. At this point, you are officially the owner of the property.

The major difference between the two? The closing around the table can open up the possibility for the other party (or you) to reopen a negotiation session. If the other party knows that you have taken irrevocable steps to move, he may try to blackmail you into last-minute concessions. There-

> Keep the final closing statement for income tax reasons. Some of the items on the HUD-1 statement are tax-deductible.

fore, it's critically important to have your personal attorney present at the table closing. Your attorney can provide an instructive explanation to the other side about such important concepts as *"lis pendens,"* "specific performance," and "punitive damages" for bad faith.

When escrow is opened, two players—the escrow agent and your buyer's agent—now have the ball. You or your broker's agent must make sure that all contingencies are resolved and all time deadlines are met. The coordinator at this stage is the escrow agent. She has a number of legal documents and verifications that serve as her guidelines. She must also notify various parties. These guidelines and the actions needed are listed as follows:

1. Written instructions from you and the seller
2. The sales contract containing contingencies and deadlines
3. Title insurance commitment or abstract of title
4. Lender's closing instructions

5. Verification of repairs and other actions specified in written instructions
6. Verification of receipt and delivery of funds from different sources
7. Verification of delivery of insurances for different purposes specified in written instructions
8. Notification to different government agencies for recording, tax, and other purposes

The closing can last for several hours or be resolved in less than an hour. It all depends on how prepared you are. You'll need to produce a certified check for closing. Bring along a checkbook to pay for legitimate charges that may come up. Be ready for intimidating pressure from a lot of people to "get on with it" and sign all the documents. Even though you are committing yourself to thirty years of payments, the other people at the closing will put pressure on you to sign quickly without reading or having all the documents explained to your satisfaction. Remember, the deal is not done until you sign, so enjoy your moment of power.

> The deal is not done until you sign, so enjoy your moment of power.

This is also your last opportunity to ask any questions. You should have already read most of the documents and had them explained to you by your lawyer (ideally) or your broker's agent (less than ideally).

The closing will be supervised by the lender, escrow agent, title company officer, closing attorney, or builder's agent. The exact person and procedure varies. Most closings go smoothly; however, even the most organized closings can include mistakes. You can reduce mistakes, especially "intentional mistakes" that can cost you money, in a number of ways. Here are eight recommendations:

1. Meet your escrow officer ahead of time. Introduce yourself and ask if you can do anything to make the closing more efficient. If the escrow agent gets to know you personally, it's likely she'll take more care in preparing your documentation.

2. Read as much of the paperwork as possible in advance of the closing and have your lawyer review this paperwork. Try to resolve all problems before you go to closing.

3. By law the lender must make the final settlement statement available to you one business day before closing. Advise the lender in advance that you and your attorney need to read this statement and schedule a time you can come by and pick it up.

4. Arrange for the closing to take place in the afternoon so you have time to do your final walk-through in the morning. Bring your plastic box with the documents you've been sent or received. You want this at the closing just in case you have to refer to these items. Also, bring a calculator and a sharp pencil.

5. Bring your attorney along to the closing. If the lender and escrow officer have been advised that your attorney will be accompanying you to the closing, it is more likely that everything will go smoothly.

6. Ask the escrow officer to walk you through each document and to explain the numbers. Check these numbers with the HUD Settlement Statement you picked up the day before.

7. Ask for an explanation of any discrepancies between the good faith estimate and the final figures in the set-

tlement statement. Complain and ask for surprise processing fees and "warehouse" fees to be cancelled.

8. Be prepared to walk out if discrepancies cannot be satisfactorily explained or resolved. Because you may have been waiting for many weeks for the closing, you may be reluctant to do this, especially if it's for some minor charge. If your attorney is not present at the closing, make a phone call to your attorney and ask the closing officer to explain the discrepancy to him.

 ## IT'S MOVING DAY!

Moving can be very hectic. It's a time for screaming and yelling and crying. It's also a time for excitement and joy. However, if you have a competent mover, the packing, moving, and unpacking will be simplified. You should have already changed your mailing address and taken other steps mentioned earlier in this chapter to get ready to move. Once the house is yours, you still have a number of things you should do as you move in. These include the following:

1. Arrange for any utilities to be hooked up.

2. Change all of the locks and security codes. Check all windows and doors for their safety.

3. Put up curtains or blinds to create privacy and discourage burglars from casing the place.

4. Make sure the deed has been recorded. Ask your escrow agent to confirm that this has been done.

5. Apply for any homestead exemptions available to reduce property taxes.

6. Correct your address on your driver's license, or if you've moved from another state, get a new state license and register to vote.

7. Make a punch list of items that need repair and are covered by your homeowner's warranty.

8. Pay extra attention to your children. It may take several weeks before they are accustomed to their new surroundings and new school environment.

9. Meet your neighbors.

10. Invite your real estate agent over for lunch or a drink and thank her for her efforts. Now is the time you can create a real friendship.

If you have closed the transaction and moved into your house, you have taken the final step and are now a homeowner. Congratulations!

8

Five Stories
of Success

This chapter contains five stories, or case studies, of successful home-buying strategies. Four of these stories are based on real-life experiences, but people and places are slightly disguised. Following each story is a brief commentary on how you can use the example to help you with your home-buying experience.

A common problem people face when they decide to buy a home is the lack of sufficient money for a down payment. Unfortunately, most Americans don't save money directly. Instead, most of our savings is in the form of 401(k) and corporate retirement plans, which cannot be easily accessed. Therefore, many new homebuyers need to receive gifts from parents, make special arrangements with their employers, or seek financial contributions from motivated sellers. However, those who use these means are under stricter scrutiny by the lender. There are several alternatives, including many government programs that have low or no down payments and low closing costs for qualified individuals. Some special low-income programs even allow the borrower to substitute "sweat equity" instead of cash. This refers to the labor and time that one puts into the improvement of a house.

The following story is an example of how sweat equity allowed an enterprising young man to acquire a very expensive house that he could not have bought in a traditional way.

JUAN'S STORY: A HELPING HAND FROM A HELPFUL HANDYMAN

Juan was poor but resourceful. He was planning to get married and start a family. But first, as a matter of pride, he felt he had to have a house. The problem was he had no money for a down payment. Although Juan had few financial resources, his human resources were vast. He could fix virtually everything from toasters to furnaces. Juan, who had worked as a ditch digger, a carpenter, an electrician's helper, and a plumber's assistant, was also not afraid to work long hours.

He was sitting in a college night class when his city planning professor mentioned that he was thinking of selling his old house and rebuilding another house in a more strategically located neighborhood. The professor discussed a problem he had. How could he finance the reconstruction of the second house without selling his first house? He and his family still needed to live somewhere before the second house was finished. The professor said that if he couldn't solve that problem, he might have to drop the whole idea. This got Juan thinking. The next day he made the professor an offer he couldn't refuse.

> A common problem people face when they decide to buy a home is the lack of sufficient money for a down payment.

Juan offered to buy the house if he could assume the mortgage. Instead of making a down payment, Juan promised to work 1,000 hours in helping the professor reconstruct the other house. To sweeten the deal, Juan promised to let the professor live in his original house rent-free until the other house was finished. The only stipulation was that Juan was also going to be renovating the professor's original house. The professor had to agree in the written contract that Juan could move the professor's family out of their rooms into other rooms when the time came to renovate them. Juan pointed out the following advantages:

1. The professor would save on a real estate commission and other closing costs.

2. The professor would be freed of his primary obligation on his mortgage loan and thus eligible for a new loan to buy and renovate the other house.

3. The professor would have Juan, an experienced builder, to supervise the rehabilitation of the professor's other house (Juan embellished his experience).

4. The professor would be able to live in his old house rent-free.

5. Juan would take the house as is and without any contingencies or requirements for surveys or title searches. This would save the professor money.

6. The professor would be able to buy and renovate his other house immediately without waiting a long time for his existing house to be sold at some unknown price.

Juan benefited because he didn't have to qualify for a new loan. His "sweat equity" would substitute for a cash down payment. He would have a place to live without paying rent.

After contemplating the offer, the professor accepted and signed Juan's contract. The professor was soon to regret his bargain. Juan proved that sometimes students are smarter than their professors. Juan placed a higher priority on renovating the professor's old house than on renovating the professor's new house. Several times the professor's family had to move their bedrooms. The professor was surprised when Juan stated that while the professor and his family could stay, most of the furniture had to be removed because it was interfering with the renovation. This was a right that Juan's lawyer had included in the contract but that the professor had not read. Finally, the straw that broke the camel's back was when Juan hired a number of low-paid transient workers to complete the 1,000 hours owed. The contract did not state that Juan was "personally" responsible for putting in the hours but just that he was responsible for having 1,000 hours of labor performed. The professor was saddened by the fact that he had already given Juan an "A" for the planning course he had previously taken.

> Creativity can overcome big obstacles.

Comment: Although the names and city are disguised, Juan's story actually happened. The story points out that creativity can overcome big obstacles. When "Juan" was able to arrange the deal, he had no job and was a full-time graduate student. After he had completed the reconditioning and rehabilitation of the house, he was able to successfully sell it for more than triple the mortgage loan he had assumed. In my estimation, in addition to not having any down payment, Juan was also able to buy the house at a significant discount. The story also holds a warning about mixing business with friendship.

The eight-step strategy presented in this book works well in normal markets and exceedingly well in buyer's markets. However, many of the rules for searching and negotiations do not apply in seller's markets. The following story provides an illustration of a tactic that was successfully used to acquire a home in a hot seller's market.

CHAN'S STORY: THE FIVE-OFFER ACCEPTANCE

Chan was very frustrated. The weather was extremely hot, the market was very hot, and Chan was getting hot under the collar. He had been transferred to a city in a Western state that was experiencing a real estate boom. Prices were escalating every day as buyers struggled to bid up prices to tempt sellers to sell. Builders even had to hold lotteries to provide the multitude of buyers with a chance to buy their new homes.

Previously, Chan had lived in the area of the Midwest called the "rust belt" because of the many factories that had closed within the past twenty years. He had left a real estate market that had many sellers and few buyers. Fortunately, his corporate relocation program had bought his house for the same price he had originally purchased it for five years before. Otherwise he would have had to take a loss. Meanwhile, Chan and his wife were staying at a motel.

Two real estate agents, acting as a team, had been working with Chan for the past two weeks. Many times they had found a perfect house; however, ignoring the advice of his sales team, he had insisted on making a lowball offer. These offers were, of course, refused. Finally, Chan learned his lesson and started making full-price offers. Unfortunately, these, too, were turned down—either because he waited too long to make up his mind or some other buyer had outbid him. He didn't know what to do.

This had been another day of offers and rejections. Chan and his wife had left their real estate agents earlier and planned to meet with them at 5:00 P.M. the next day, after Chan finished work. The agents had a list of five houses or condominiums that they planned to visit. These had been carefully selected from a much larger list of choices. Chan and his wife had dinner that night at the Maple Garden, a Chinese restaurant, to plan strategy. While looking over the menu, he noticed several items had names that included the number five, such as "five-spice chicken," "five-flavor hot and sour soup," and "five-seafood egg rolls." He thought about the meaning of this. Tomorrow was May 5. Chan suddenly realized that tomorrow the number five was important. He told his wife, "I know what we will do. I will get a five-offer acceptance." After dinner, he called his real estate brokers and told them to prepare an offer on each of the properties. He insisted that each offer include the number "5" and that a contingency would state that the contract was subject to a "satisfactory" inspection.

The next day, Chan visited the first condominium. It was on the water in a complex with a swimming pool and a tennis court. His agents left his written offer of $485,000. The next offering was a home located on a golf course. The offer for this was $550,000. The third selection was a condominium on an island in the middle of a lake with a small bridge connecting it to the mainland. This property required extensive restoration because it suffered from mildew damage. Chan made a lowball offer of $185,500. The fourth property was a pole house on a hill with a spectacular view of a bay filled with sailboats. Chan made an offer of $350,000 for the property. The fifth property, a townhouse condominium on the eighteenth fairway of a golf course, was priced at $290,000. Chan decided to add 55 cents to the listing price and made an offer of $290,000.55.

> The successful buyer was able to spend time inspecting each of the houses thoroughly and used the contingency inspection clause to cancel the other two contracts, with a full refund of the earnest money payment.

Later that night, his real estate agents called Chan. All his offers except the fifth one had been turned down. He had outbid five other buyers who were making offers—by only 55 cents. He and his wife bought the house and moved in. They also joined the golf club. On May 5 the following year, Chan made his first hole-in-one. Yes, you probably guessed—it was on the fifth hole.

Comment: Two things are not true about the story. Out of the five simultaneous offers, three were actually accepted instead of just one. The successful buyer was able to spend time inspecting each of the houses thoroughly and used the contingency inspection clause to cancel the other two contracts, with a full refund of the earnest money payment. The other exaggeration is the hole-in-one. "Chan" has yet to break a hundred. It was "Chan's" wife who scored the hole-in-one—twice.

Some people never buy a house because they cannot accumulate enough money to make an offer on the house they really want. Other people have discovered the "move-up" strategy. They buy a house that they can afford and live there while their equity builds up. When they sell the first house, they then have enough equity to buy a better house. The equity builds from both the appreciation of the house and the reduction of the mortgage balance. It may take two or three of these stages before they are able to finally move into their dream home. Lydia's story is an example of how the move-up strategy worked in just one step.

 ## LYDIA'S STORY: FIXING THE NEST TO FINANCE A NEST EGG

When Lydia L. was a little girl, she dreamed of owning a large house with its own garden and a white picket fence. Unfortunately, as an adult she couldn't afford her dream house. What was worse, the more she and her husband saved, the more impossible her dream home seemed. By the time she had saved $1,000, her dream home had increased in price by $10,000. The monthly rental check was just more money going out the door. She now had a little girl of her own—an additional reason to dream about her house.

Lydia came to see me after one of my classes and explained her problem. She and her husband had $10,000 in savings. This was not enough for her to make a down payment on the house she wanted. I suggested that she needed leverage to build up her down payment. "Buy a house you can afford and build up your equity. Find a fixer-upper with cosmetic problems but no serious structural or mechanical problems," I advised. "There is a neighborhood in town that is undergoing major restoration. You might want to look there." At that time, this metropolitan city was building a rapid transit system and urban pioneers were fixing up a few neighborhoods. I thought Lydia was well suited to be one of these pioneers.

> Some people never buy a house because they cannot accumulate enough money to make an offer on the house they really want.

Lydia and her husband found a small Victorian house in a neighborhood that was only a five-minute drive from the downtown area. They were able to get a government-insured loan with a down payment and closing costs of approximately $5,000, including a $1500 down payment. They spent about a year redoing the house. During that time, the value of the houses in the neighborhood increased by 30%. The following year, there was another increase of about 25%. The third year saw an additional increase of 10%. However, Lydia's house appreciated even more because she had used her innate good taste to turn a run-down fixer-upper into a Victorian jewel. After three years they sold the house to a professional couple who worked downtown.

Here's how Lydia's family's net worth changed because of her investment in the house:

Starting net worth:　　$10,000 in savings

Beginning of Year 1
Investment in house:　$50,000
Mortgage:　　　　　－ 48,500
Equity in house:　　　$ 1,500
Closing costs:　　　　－$ 3,500

After they bought their house, their net worth dropped to $6,500. This is based on the $5,000 they had remaining in savings and the $1,500 equity they had in the house. That year they spent $10,000 remodeling. To do this they had to cut unnecessary entertainment expenses. Remodeling the home was their new entertainment. After the remodeling, the house was worth $78,000. Their savings were almost depleted, so their net worth was just the equity they had in the house. This is calculated as follows:

Beginning of Year 2

Market value:	$78,000
Mortgage balance:	− 48,007
Equity:	$29,993

During the second year, they put another $10,000 into remodeling. Their house now had a market value of $110,000.

Beginning of Year 3

Market value:	$110,000
Mortgage balance:	− 47,479
Equity:	$ 62,521

Again, they put $10,000 in remodeling. Their house was now worth $132,000. They decided to sell it because both had finished their education programs and were moving to another town. Here's what they had after they sold the house:

Sales price:	$132,000
Transaction costs:	− 10,560
Mortgage balance:	− 46,912
Net proceeds:	$ 74,528

After just three years, Lydia and her husband had nearly $75,000 to put down on Lydia's large dream house with its own garden and a white picket fence. Without having bought their first house, they would still be renting and dreaming.

Comment: This story is representative of many people I have known. The move-up strategy works well in normal markets and normal neighborhoods. It works spectacularly well in neighborhoods that undergo "gentrification." In the normal neighborhood life cycle, many neighborhoods begin to decline as the housing gets old and begins to deteriorate. Throughout the United States, primarily in the inner city of large metropolitan areas, some neighborhoods begin to renew themselves. These neighborhoods are typically characterized by great locations with easy access to the central business district, well-built and well-designed houses that have stood the test of time, a well-planned neighborhood with public parks and sidewalks, initial low prices of the houses, and the catalyst of some imaginative, risk-taking, and persistent pioneers.

> The move-up strategy works well in normal markets and normal neighborhoods.

One of the difficulties most consumers face is comparing the relative cost of different kinds of mortgage products. The federal government has tried to help consumers by requiring lenders to disclose the APR and finance charges. The APR is a rule-of-thumb calculation that can lead to sub-optimal consumer choices. However, tools are available on the Internet that provide a solution. Consider Judy's story.

JUDY'S STORY: HERE COME DA JUDGE

Judy K. was perplexed. She was judging three mortgage loan products for a house she had agreed to purchase. The agreed-to price was $100,000. She was offered the following terms:

	Mortgage A	Mortgage B	Mortgage C
Down payment	5%	20%	20%
Monthly payments	$906.93	$552.54	$545.74
Interest rate	7%	7.375%	7.25%
Points	3 points	2 points	3 points
Term	15 years	30 years	30 years
Closing costs	$2,850	$2,400	$2,400

The three mortgage products she was considering had different down payments, monthly payments, interest rates, points, terms, and closing costs. She wanted to pay the lowest interest rate possible. Initially, she judged the contract interest rate. On that basis, Mortgage A was the best. However, the monthly payments were much higher and she didn't really want to pay the higher closing costs.

	Mortgage A	Mortgage B	Mortgage C
Interest rate	7%	7.375%	7.25%
Rank	1	3	2

Judy's lender provided her with an estimate of the APR for each loan. Disclosure of the APR is required under the Truth in Lending law. On that basis, Mortgage A was actually the worst and Mortgage C was the best. Her lender advised her that the APR was not necessarily her true cost. If she paid off her loan early, the true cost would increase. He also told her that her income tax bracket had an impact on her true cost after tax. If she wanted to discover her true cost, she could call her accountant or her financial advisor.

	Mortgage A	Mortgage B	Mortgage C
Estimated APR	7.9498%	7.8770%	7.8467%
Rank	3	2	1

Judy was too frugal to pay out big bucks to have someone tell her what the cheapest mortgage was. Instead, she checked the Internet and found the "True Cost Calculator" Web site made available by Fannie Mae (www.homepath

.com). The Web site let her specify her mortgage terms and how long she planned to keep the loan. She planned to sell the property after seven years. On this basis she found that the lowest cost mortgage was actually Mortgage B.

	Mortgage A	Mortgage B	Mortgage C
True cost rate	8.86%	8.35%	8.43%
Rank	3	1	2

When Judy put in her estimated tax bracket of 31%, the ranking did not change. She was gratified, however, that her after-tax true cost was as low as 5.88%.

	Mortgage A	Mortgage B	Mortgage C
True cost rate after tax	6.39%	5.88%	5.92%
Rank	3	1	2

On the basis of the new information she received that was calculated on her personal circumstances, she was able to select Mortgage B as her lowest-cost loan.

Comment: Judy is a completely fictitious character used to help personalize the use of "The True Cost Calculator" on the Internet. Fannie Mae is the Federal National Mortgage Association. Unlike many of the Internet sites that are touting their own mortgage loans, Fannie Mae's does not have a commercial bias. Fannie Mae provides a tool for evaluating a broad range of fixed-rate and ARM loans based on a person's tax circumstances and plans for future moves.

The final story shows how imagination and action can create entrepreneurial wealth for the savvy homebuyer.

JERRY'S STORY:
WORK HARD AND GET A FREE CONDO

I hadn't seen Jerry K. for years, yet there he was sitting next to me in tourist class flying to London. He had been my graduate assistant many years ago, and I asked what he was doing now. He was working for himself, investing in real estate. I asked him how he had gotten started after he dropped out of the graduate program.

Jerry had moved to South City, U.S.A., where he found a comfortable townhouse apartment within walking distance from the fancy downtown hotel where he worked at the bar. He and his roommate shared the $850-per-month rent on a two bedroom, 1½-bath unit with a kitchen, a dining area, and a living/dining room. It was part of an eight-unit townhouse-style building that was attractively landscaped. Including tips, Jerry made approximately $42,000 each year. Jerry was also trying to be a writer. This was at least his fifth or sixth career move of which I was aware.

His comfortable world was disrupted when the landlord gave notice to everybody that he was putting his eight-unit apartment unit up for sale. The listing price was $680,000. The notice advised each tenant that when the project was sold, they would have to move unless they signed new leases with the future owner. Jerry calculated the average price for each unit to be $85,000—100 times the monthly rent.

When he started looking for a new place, he discovered that similar units in the same neighborhood were renting for from $1,050 to $1,200 per month. The more expensive units had access to swimming pools. Just for kicks, he decided to see how much condominium units were selling for elsewhere. He was surprised to learn that similar units were going for from $150,000 to $160,000 for two-bedroom, one-full-bath properties.

Jerry did a comparison of whether he should rent or buy. (To reproduce his reasoning, the "Rent vs. Buy" comparison calculator for "Quicken Loans" was used (see chapter 9 or visit Quicken.com).

Jerry's financial assumptions were input into the calculator:

Monthly rent payment: $1,050
Purchase price: $150,000

Down payment (5%):	$7,500
Gross income:	$42,000
Estimated stay in house:	7 years
Tax filing status:	Single

Jerry actually didn't have the $7,500, but he thought he might be able to raise it. He only had about $1,500 in his checking account. Here's a summary of the output:

Short-Term Cost Comparison:	Rent	Buy
Monthly payment:	$ 1,050	$ 1,176
Average monthly tax savings:	$ 0	$ 326
After-tax monthly payment:	$ 1,050	$ 850
Total cost over the next 7 years:	$119,024	$48,898

Jerry realized that if he bought a unit similar to the one he was renting, he would pay exactly the same amount in after-tax mortgage payments as he was paying for his current rent. But if he had to move and pay the higher market rent of $1,050, he would have to pay an additional $300 out of pocket each month. What really surprised Jerry was how much money he would save in the long run by buying instead of renting. The calculator computed that Jerry would save $70,126 in total cost over the next seven years.

Jerry's big problem was he didn't have the down payment, his credit was terrible because of his bartending job, and his roommate was planning to leave for Las Vegas. Jerry's other option was to move to a less desirable neighborhood, which he really didn't want to do. Jerry had an inspiration. Although he couldn't qualify to buy a single unit, he might be able to buy an entire building!

He called one of his frequent customers, a real estate lawyer. The lawyer agreed to do all the paperwork necessary to buy the building, create a condominium regime, and provide other legal advice for $5,000 and free drinks on Fridays for an entire year. (Jerry arranged this with his boss by agreeing to reimburse the bar.) He also talked to some of his friends who were in the remodeling business and found that he could get them to remodel each unit with new paint, carpeting, light fixtures, and new appliances for from $8,000 to $10,000 per unit. They agreed to commit to this price in writing for ninety days.

He then talked to his neighbors, asking that if he could show them how they could stay in their present units, have the units remodeled, pay the same after-tax housing expenses, and end up owning the units, would they be interested? He also showed them how they would save over $70,000 during the next seven years. Six of the seven neighbors said they would. Jerry had them sign conditional contracts indicating their willingness to buy if he could deliver on his promises.

Jerry approached the owner and made a full-price offer. The offer was subject to a financing condition. He realized later that he should have negotiated, but this was his first real estate purchase and he didn't want to lose it. He also didn't want the seller to check into his financial condition and hoped that a little greed would cause the landlord to be a little careless.

Not surprisingly, many of his customers at the bar were bankers. He decided he needed interim financing of $850,000 for no more than ninety days. He provided one of his banking friends with the following financial statement:

Revenues (6 sales @ $150,000 each)	$900,000
Purchase price	$680,000
Condo/legal fees	$5,000
Appliances/fixtures/carpets/labor	$72,000
Contribution to buyer's closing costs	$54,000
Loan fees/interest on interim loan	$25,000
Miscellaneous/reserves	$10,000
Gross profit	$54,000
Taxes	$16,000
After-tax profits	$38,000

The banker saw the financial pro-forma. He was impressed with the signed contracts. After running a credit check on each of the potential buyers, the banker agreed to make the loan.

One of the buyers dropped out when he realized how much money Jerry was making, but someone else was quickly found to take his place. Jerry did not renew the lease of the one neighbor who didn't want to buy. He used this unit for the buyers to temporarily use while he remodeled their units.

The entire process took less than two months. When it was over, Jerry owned his personal unit free and clear. He kept the unsold unit as a rental property that he leased at $1,050 per month. This grossed him $12,600 each year. He also ended up with about $35,000 in the bank. This was after spending over $1,000 to keep a lawyer inebriated for fifty-two Fridays in a row. Jerry marveled that the lawyer didn't miss a single Friday.

At the time I sat with Jerry on the plane, he owned several apartment rental units in the best part of town. I asked Jerry why he wasn't flying first class? He replied that he was cheap. He was still living in that condo that he got for free for all his hard work.

Comment: Jerry K. is actually a synthesis of two different people I have known. The former graduate student I met on the airplane to London did not do the condominium conversion deal. His story is almost as interesting. He began his adventure to real estate wealth when he was evicted from an apartment for not paying his rent. Rather than letting him live on the streets, his parents lent him enough money to buy a duplex. He fixed up the duplex, sold it, and bought an eight-unit apartment building. This he pyramided into a twenty-four-unit apartment building, and eventually he owned several hundred units. The person who pulled off the condominium conversion deal eventually became a successful college professor. The story is important because it shows that by proper sequencing, it is possible to satisfy the needs of a lender, the customers, and the seller of a property.

9

Using the Internet

The Internet is an amazing free library of information and tools that allow you to gather information—and even analyze it so you can make a better home-buying decision. I have listed some Web sites that will help make your home-buying process more effective. A rating scale is included to help you judge the merit of these sites. Here's how the ratings work.

Home-Buying Web Site Rating Description/Rating

Web sites rated with five houses are indispensable to the home-buying process. These sites provide key tools and information. They also allow you to easily custom design information for your own use.

Web sites rated with four houses are excellent but not indispensable. There may be alternative ways of developing the information.

Web sites rated with three houses are good but are often difficult to use and understand. They may also have a clear commercial bias encouraging you to use the services of the site provider.

Web sites rated with two houses are fair, providing some information. However, they can be misleading without a full understanding of real estate and the buying process. Usually, calculations are "rules of thumb" applying to the general public but not specifically designed for your particular needs.

A Web site rated with one house provides information that may or may not be useful but may be one of a few sites that provides that category of information or services. These sites should be used with caution.

SEARCH ENGINES

Besides the few Web sites listed in this chapter, millions of others provide valuable information. Using the search engines on the World Wide Web, you can access the best of these quickly and efficiently. Two search engines I regularly use are Google and Dogpile. I'll start with Google because I usually find what I need there without my having to resort to Dogpile.

Google

Address: http://www.google.com

Buying Decision: Not applicable

What It Does: Google finds relevant Web sites directly based on the words you put into the search engine. You can specify the language the search should focus on, and Google is able to provide an automatic translation into English for many of the foreign Web sites it finds.

Example: In the space provided, type "mortgage loans" and click on "Google Search." This will result in a display of the first ten out of over two billion Web sites it has found. At the end of the listing is: 1 2 3 4 5 6 7 8 9 10 NEXT. If you click on 2, the next 10 listings will be displayed, and so on.

Dogpile

Address: http://www.dogpile.com

Buying Decision: Not applicable

What It Does: Dogpile is a meta-search engine that searches approximately fifteen other search engines or directories, including Yahoo. Some of these search engines display a lot of junk Web sites, making the Dogpile search less efficient.

Example: In the space provided, type "mortgage loans" and click on "Fetch." Typically, a display ad will pop up along with a list displaying the top finds of a couple of search engines. You have the option of getting more from a specific search engine, or you can choose to see additional search engines.

GENERAL REAL ESTATE SERVICES AGGREGATION SITES

Aggregation sites are designed to attract large numbers of looks for the purpose of redirecting them through a "one-click" step to other real estate services. Each of the sites selected in this section average over three million unique visitors each month.

HomeAdvisor

Address: http://www.homeadvisor.msn.com

Buying Decision: All major decisions are covered.

What It Does: HomeAdvisor covers many hyperlinked sites pertinent to the home-buying process, including these topics: home listings, find an agent, compare cities, neighborhoods, insurance center, virtual tours, brand new homes, city finder, cost of living, your first home, apply for a loan, and others.

Examples:

1. On the home page, look for a feature called "Find Homes for Sale." It allows you to specify a price range and a ZIP code. After you press "Go," you are

given your "home search results." I tried the ZIP code where I grew up and found 160 houses listed, ranked by price from lowest to highest. The program allows you to further specify number of bedrooms and baths. The screen also allows you to store your favorite homes and get placed on a free e-mail service to advise you of new listings.

2. By clicking on "Neighborhoods" under "Find Homes for Sales," you can specify a state, a region, median home costs, median age of homes, and property crime risk. For example, if you want a neighborhood with a low crime rate, you can specify this. I tried looking for areas with a low crime rate in one city and found only four neighborhoods. When I selected "high crime rate," I was given a list of twenty-seven neighborhoods.

3. Another nice feature on the home page is your ability to input a street address and a ZIP code to find out how much your house is worth. The result will give a price range. In some cases, you may instead get an estimate based on neighborhood growth rates if you enter the price and the date when you bought your house.

HomeStore

Address: http://www.homestore.com

Buying Decision: All major decisions are covered.

What It Does: On the HomeStore site, you can choose separate hyperlinks for previously owned homes, new homes, manufactured homes, and specialized communities of senior living. For previously owned homes, you are automatically hyperlinked to the REALTOR.com site. You'll find a prominent place on the home page for mortgage financing as well as tools including a primitive mortgage payment calculator and calculators for "Home Affordability," "Rent vs. Buy," and "Compare Cost of Living."

Examples:

    1. On the home page, click on "Local Coupon" under "Welcome Wagon." This will bring you to "Find Local Merchants and Services." Input your ZIP code and a radius of from five to twenty miles. Click "Go." You will get a list of merchants that includes a coupon and a map locating the merchant that you can print out.

    2. If you click on "Rent vs. Buy," then on "Compare Cost of Living," you can choose to "Browse Categories." This has a list of reports and a wide variety of calculators. If you press school reports, you will be asked to select a state, then a city. At this point, you will get a summary table of all the school districts in the city, giving you student-teacher ratio, average class size, and a few other statistics. You can then get a detailed report on each school district listing SAT scores, percentage of students going to college, awards and recognitions, and much more. To get this free report, you must fill in an online application giving personal details. The report will be created online, but "The sponsor(s) you check will contact you with more information and money saving offer(s)."

REALTOR.com

Address: http://www.realtor.com

Buying Decision: All major decisions are covered.

What It Does: The main menu at this site allows you to select from "Neighborhoods," "Properties by Category," "Mortgage and Finance," "Find a Lender," "Check Home Sales Prices," "Tools," and other pertinent hyperlinks. Also useful is a very prominent display of "Today's Interest Rates" for the 30-year fixed, the 15-year fixed, and the 1-year ARM.

Examples:

    1. On the home page, click on "Check Home Sale Prices." You will be asked to input the street address, city, state, or ZIP code and to indicate whether you

want recent sales "on the entire street," "in this neighborhood," or "just this address." You will also be asked what years you want included (for example: "From 1987 to 2001"). Click on "Get Prices." You will get a list of all homes sold during the time period specified and the dates they sold. Some states like Texas are "nondisclosure" states, so you will not be provided with this information.

2. On the home page, click on "Find a REALTOR." You will be asked to indicate a city and state or province or indicate a ZIP code. Options include specifying REALTORS with Web sites and REALTORS who specialize in helping buyers. One of my favorite features is the option to specify REALTORS who have any of sixteen professional designations and certifications.

3. On the home page, click on "Neighborhoods." Under "Find Neighborhood," you will insert the ZIP code. By clicking "Go," you will get a neighborhood map and detailed information about schools, crime, and average home qualities. You can then find homes in the neighborhood by clicking "Go" in answer to the command to "Show me homes in this ZIP code." You are then taken to a page where you can specify the features of the home you are seeking from a list of nearly seventy choices.

SEX OFFENDERS

You can find many Web sites on sex offender registries, motivated by "Megan's Law." A Google search will find registries that are specific to your state. The following is one of the better national sites. It will direct you to state registries and provide additional information focused on protecting your children.

Stop Sex Offender!
Address: http://www.stopsexoffenders.com

Buying Decision: Investigating your neighborhood for dangers

What It Does: Stop Sex Offender! Provides a wide variety of information on child safety issues, such as school bullies, babysitters, school safety, stalking, and senior safety. You can also bring up a sex offender registry by selecting your state. You are then taken to the official state registry, if this is available online. However, some states, such as California, require you to visit a police or sheriff's office to access the information from a CD while you are there. The typical information in the registry includes a picture of the sex offender and where he or she lives.

> Some states, such as California, require you to visit a police or sheriff's office to access information about sex offenders.

Example: The "Child Safety" section contains a number of valuable tools, including a form you can download called the "Child Identification System." It allows you to record important information about your child, such as blood type, and includes space for fingerprints and for the child's photo. You can also print and fill in a "Pocket Child ID" card that your child can keep with him or her. If your child is ever lost, he or she can be quickly reunited with you.

 ## HAZARDOUS WASTE

The best information on this topic comes from the EPA. The "Love Canal" incident has made everybody more aware of the dangers of toxic wastes hidden in their own neighborhoods. We know that environmental dangers can pose an especially serious problem for young children during their developmental stages.

U.S. Environmental Protection Agency
Address: http://www.epa.gov/epahome
Buying Decision: Neighborhood and area environmental hazards
What It Does: This is a comprehensive site on the types of hazards that are regulated by the EPA. When I accessed this site, it contained a great deal of topical information about the World Trade Center and Pentagon tragedies, including steps being taken to monitor asbestos and particulate matter in New York. The site is a little crowded but has a handy search function.
Example: Type "superfund sites" in the search function on the home page. You will be taken directly to a listing by state of superfund hazard sites. Click on your state to find addresses of the problem sites.

 # FINDING A HOME INSPECTOR

A recent Google search revealed about 350,000 Web sites that deal with home inspection. The first site listed was the official home page of the American Society of Home Inspectors. This is also one of the best.

American Society of Home Inspectors (ASHI)
Address: http://www.ashi.org
Buying Decision: Getting your home inspected
What It Does: Helps you find a certified home inspector.
Example: Click on "Find an inspector." You will be asked to input your ZIP code and the distance from your home in which you want to limit your search. A list of certified inspectors is provided, including their telephone numbers, e-mail addresses, and, in a few cases, Web site addresses.

 # SELECTING A FLOOR PLAN

Various Web sites allow you to select a floor plan design or buy a software package to help you with your own design.

After reviewing many of these, I selected the following site for its user-friendly interface.

eplans.com The Houseplan Superstore

Address: http://www.eplans.com

Buying Decision: Evaluating floor plans for possible ideas of what you might want to look for in an existing home or one that is custom built

What It Does: Allows you to identify house plans based on custom-selected criteria. The Web site has a quick search function and a custom-design function. The purpose of the site is to sell you plans, but I like to use it for possible ideas.

Example: Click on "Search our home plan blueprints database today." You will be asked to specify square footage, number of bedrooms and baths, architectural design styles, lifestyle features, foundation type, number of floors, garage size, and other information. After you submit your search, you will see a number of pictures of what the houses look like, some features, and an estimated national cost to build. By clicking on the picture, you will get floor plans and more information.

APPRAISING A HOUSE

There is no real substitute for a professional appraisal. However, the Internet can provide some ballpark figures for house values. The following Web site gives you a reasonable value of the cost of building a house in your city. It does not give you the land value. To come up with a ballpark estimate of property value, you will need to add the results of this Web site to the value of a developable site in your neighborhood.

Building-Cost.net

Address: http://www.building-cost.net

Buying Decision: Appraising the cost of the improvements/insurance

What It Does: This is a very sophisticated yet easy to use calculator. It estimates the cost of building a wide variety of houses in specific ZIP codes. This is one of the most impressive calculators I have viewed. But you need to know how to calibrate the numbers that are based on quality. I had to move up one level to equate proper values for my market. This means that, unless you know what the local market numbers are, you should use this calculator with great caution. The site deserves a "⌂⌂⌂⌂⌂" rating, but I awarded it a "⌂⌂⌂⌂." This is because a consumer unaware of market conditions is likely to misinterpret the results.

> Building-Cost.net gives you a reasonable value of the cost of building a house in your city.

Example: When you reach the home page, click on "Start Calculator." You will be asked to specify the number of corners in your house. You will then be led through a series of questions about the total living area; quality class of eleven components; details about attic, balcony, basement, garage; and other information. Other questions will follow about location of house, fireplaces, multistory homes, state, and ZIP code. You will then be provided with a very detailed set of costs by item, including labor, material, and equipment used in each item.

FINDING A LAWYER

Martindale-Hubble has been a national publisher of lawyer directories for generations. Their Web site is a quick way to narrow down lawyers to those who claim a practice specialty that might be of interest. The site does not assure you that the attorneys on the list are trustworthy. You will have to verify this to your own satisfaction by interviewing prospects and checking references.

Martindale-Hubbell Lawyer Locator
Address: http://www.martindale.com
Buying Decision: Selecting a lawyer to advise you
What It Does: Does a database search that allows you to identify a list of lawyers by specialty who are practicing in your state.
Example: Go to the home page and select the tab that says "Location/Area of Practice"; otherwise, you will get a list of all lawyers in the state. Scrolling down practice areas, select "Real Estate." Put in the city and state. Be sure to spell the name of the city correctly. Indicate whether you have any language preference other than English. Click on "Search." You will get a list of attorneys. Click on any name and you will find specific information on that attorney, such as an address and when he or she graduated from law school. You will also get additional practice specialties. Click on "Rating Info." A lawyer will receive an "A," "B," or "C" rating for their competency, based on confidential opinions of other lawyers. A rating of "V" is bestowed on lawyers who adhere to ethical standards. Only 43% of lawyers are rated. This is not to suggest that the other lawyers are not competent or ethical. The best rating is "AV."

WEB SITES WITH CALCULATORS AND OTHER TOOLS

Web-based calculators take much of the fear and tedium out of math. You no longer have to fear making arithmetic mistakes. Computer-based calculators make it easier to make comparisons and help you make better decisions.

Quicken.com

Address: http://www.quicken.com (go to "Home Loans" on home page)

Buying Decision: Financial calculations for renting, buying, and refinancing

What It Does: Contains a number of financial calculators and opportunities for you to apply for a loan and other financial services.

Example:

1. From "Home Loans," click on "Mortgage Tools." Click on "Rates vs. Points." This allows you to compare two loans with different interest rates and different amounts of points. You are asked to specify how long you plan to stay at the house. It will then calculate which is the best loan for you and how many years you must stay for the breakeven point, which is the crossover when one loan becomes better than the other.

2. From "Mortgage Tools," click on "Rent vs. Buy." You will be asked to specify your monthly rent payment, purchase price of the house, down payment, your yearly gross income, how long you plan to stay in the house, and your tax filing status. Note that you are not asked about the type and terms of the loan you are requesting. Click on "Calculate." You will be told how much you will save if you buy. The model appears to totally ignore transaction costs, thus it should be used with great care. The rating on this calculator is "⌂."

3. From "Mortgage Tools," click on "Credit Assessment." It will ask you to answer eleven multiple-choice questions on consumer loan records, mortgage, rent, payment records, bankruptcy records, foreclosure records, and current debt collection records. As an experiment, I answered only one question in the negative. When asked whether in the last two years I had made payment "30 to 59

days" late, I answered "2 or more." This single negative answer gave me the lowest rating according to this calculator—the same rating I received when answering all eleven questions with the highest negative answers. Still, this is an interesting calculator because it focuses on the major areas that credit agencies look at. However, don't put too much reliance on it.

Fannie Mae

Address: http://www.homepath.com
Buying Decision: Evaluating different mortgages
What It Does: This is one of the most sophisticated mortgage calculators on the Internet. It is sponsored by a government agency and is objective. Its "True Cost Calculator" allows you to compare different kinds of mortgages based on your personal characteristics. Quoting from the site:

The True Cost Calculator measures four key components:
- The True Cost Rate—all the costs of a mortgage, expressed as annual percentage rate, based on how long you plan to hold the loan.
- The True Cost Rate—all the costs of a mortgage, expressed as annual percentage rate, after taking into account your potential tax savings.
- The Monthly Mortgage Payment—the amount of money you'll pay each month to your lender.
- Estimated Equity—the amount you can expect to accumulate over the life of your loan.

The Web site did not get a "☖☖☖☖☖" rating because it appears to have a glitch when it attempts to compare two mortgages. You are more likely to get meaningful results by analyzing one mortgage at a time and printing the output. Put the outputs next to each other and then compare. Once you are on the

Web site, click on "Calculators" on the green bar at the top of the page.

Example:

1. Go to "Find a Mortgage" on the Homepath home page. You will be asked to select a state. Skipping some options, the next question you need to answer is "Mortgage Type." You will have the following choices: Adjustable-Rate, Low Down Payment, Construction to Permanent, Home Improvement, Fixed-Rate, and Reverse. You will then click on "Find a Lender." A list of Fannie Mae lenders and their services is provided. This feature is rated "🏠🏠🏠🏠🏠."

2. Find the "True Cost Calculator." Indicate your plan to "Purchase a Home." Indicate you want to "Analyze One Loan." Click on "Continue." You will be asked to input home purchase price, down payment, loan type and term, interest rate, points, and whether it is an FHA loan. Click on "Calculate." You will be given the true cost of the loan based on certain assumptions. At this point, you can refine the calculated results. You will have the opportunity to change assumptions, such as the number of years before you plan to move or refinance, your tax bracket (the original calculation was 15%), and other assumptions such as whether you plan to finance the closing costs. Press "Recalculate" to find your personal "true costs."

 # QUALIFYING AND APPLYING FOR A LOAN

From approximately one-third to one-half of all new home-buyers check mortgage rates on the Internet. However, only a small fraction of borrowers actually apply for a loan online. You can usually save from one-quarter to one-half of a percentage point by comparison-shopping using the Internet. There are three kinds of lending sites:

1. Single lender sites, such as Bank of America (http:// www.bankofamerica.com)
2. Auction sites, such as LendingTree (http://www .lendingtree.com)
3. Multiple lender sites, such as E-loan (http://www .e-loan.com)

You can find many competing lender Web sites by doing a Google search. In my opinion, the auction sites are the most innovative, and we will examine one of these as a representative of what is available on the Internet.

LendingTree

Address: http://www.lendingtree.com

Buying Decision: Making a loan application

What It Does: Allows you to make an online loan application and receive up to four offers from lenders who subscribe to the LendingTree network. The home page has a wide variety of resources such as calculators, checklists, and even a SkyMiles program. You can also "Check Your Loan Status" by typing in your e-mail address and your password.

Example: To apply for a loan, click on "Start your online form now!" You will be sent to the first of six pages of an application form. The first page is titled "Tell Us About Your Loan." Many of the questions have a hypertext link called "A tip is available." Clicking on the tip gives you a short explanation about some aspect of the question being asked. At the end of the page, you'll find an electronic disclosure that you are asked to read. You must then click that you agree to electronic disclosure. If you do not agree, the questionnaire will terminate.

If you agree, the next page is headed by "Tell us about yourself." The form is easy to fill out and submit. The four quotes are a good basis for comparison-shopping—or you may accept one of these because local lenders often can't compete.

FINDING AN ESCROW COMPANY

Remember that some states use escrow to close, whereas others use attorneys who close around the table. For the second type, use the Martindale-Hubbell site to find a closing attorney. In escrow states, use a Google search to identify escrow companies. The way to do this is to type in the name of the state you live in and the word "escrow," for example, "Alabama escrow" or "California escrow." This will allow you to find a list of companies so you can shop their costs online. This is a lot more efficient than trying to shop by phone (and being on hold much of the time!). California and Washington have directories of escrow companies operating in their states. Other companies pay to be put on Web site directories. For companies on all these directories, you'll need to comparison-shop and verify each by asking the respective state's consumer protection agency about any complaints.

Escrow and Title Service.com
Address: http://www.escrowandtitleservice.com
Buying Decision: Finding an escrow company or settlement attorney
What It Does: Provides a list of self-selected escrow or title settlement service providers classified by state. Provides hyperlinks to other real estate services.
Example: Click on a state, then click on a company listed. You will be linked to that company's Web site.

CONSUMER INFORMATION WEB SITES

Two consumer sites stand out on the Internet. Both are nonprofit sites and can be counted on to be unbiased.

Real Estate Center (Texas A&M University)
Address: http://recenter.tamu.edu
Buying Decision: Consumer advice

What It Does: It provides one of the richest sources of consumer real estate information on the Internet. It provides short video clips, quizzes, and over 1,500 accessible articles in about seventy categories. The site also has a search function.

Example: Some of their recent videos include "Concrete House Safer in Tornado," "Special Loan Programs Help New Buyers," and "Water Rights: The Coming Conflict." Articles headlined on their home page have included such titles as "Black Mold: Between Hype and Hysteria," "Moving: One of Life's Stress Events," and "FHA-Insured Versus Conventional Mortgages."

HUD on your side: consumer information

Address: http://www.hud.gov/consum.cfm

Buying Decision: Consumer advice

What It Does: HUD maintains a number of boring but informative Web sites. This site is most informative for new homebuyers. The site is difficult to navigate, primarily because it tries to do too much. However, once you find the information, the effort is worthwhile. The site has sections such as "Buying a Home," "Consumer Protections Links," and a particularly good one called "Resources." It also has an "Index/Search" function. Information is provided in both English and Spanish.

Example:

1. On the home page, click on "Buying a Home." This will eventually get you to valuable and well-organized information by walking you through many of the key decision steps to buying a home. This feature of the site is rated "⌂⌂⌂⌂⌂."

2. On the home page, click on "Index/Search." You will go to a page with an index and a search function. Using the search function, type in "lead paint booklet" and click. You will go to a page called "Search Results." Look down the list and click on "Protect

Your Family from Lead in Your Home." You can then download an extremely worthwhile booklet. You are supposed to get a copy of this booklet when you are buying a house built prior to 1978. However, download and read the book even if you are buying a newer house. It could save you and your family from serious health problems.

Questions and Answers

The following are questions frequently asked by homebuyers. They are grouped by general topics that parallel the eight-step system discussed in the book. Many of your questions can be answered by using Google to search the Internet. Another Internet site that is good in answering questions is Ask Jeeves (http://www.ask.com).

 ## DECIDING TO BUY A HOME

Q. Should I buy or rent?

A. From a financial standpoint, if you're planning to move in the next two years, you should rent. If you're planning to move in three years, the answer is "maybe." If you plan to stay longer, you should seriously consider buying. Some of your reasons for buying may not be financial. For example, you may want to buy a house because your heart tells you to. That's all right, but do be aware of the ultimate cost.

Q. **What's the difference between a cooperative and a condominium?**

A. A cooperative, or co-op, is a corporation that owns a residential building. To occupy a unit in the co-op, you must buy stock in the corporation. This would entitle you to a proprietary lease. The stock and lease are personal property rights, and you would be subject to eviction for violating rules under the lease. If you buy a condominium or condo, you own real property. You hold individual ownership in your own unit and joint ownership in the common areas.

> If you plan to stay longer than three years in one location, you should seriously consider buying.

Q. **What's the difference between a condominium and a townhouse?**

A. A townhouse is just like a condominium except that you own the land underneath your building unit.

Q. **What is a Community Association?**

A. A community association is an entity run by a board of directors elected by homeowners in a community or condominium. It manages amenities such as a swimming pool and maintains the common areas. It also enforces the CC&Rs.

Q. **What are CC&Rs?**

A. CC&Rs are covenants, conditions, and restrictions. CC&Rs are characteristic of most modern subdivisions and all condominiums. These place limitations on what the homeowner can do with her property and imposes duties to other owners in the community association.

REAL ESTATE AGENTS

Q. Won't I save money if I work without an agent?

A. No. In most cases, the seller pays the agent from the sales proceeds. As a buyer, you can get the benefits of an agent representing you and providing you with valuable advice and information for free. The exception to this is if you agree to pay a buyer's agent directly to represent you. Even in this situation, the buyer's agent may be able to negotiate the price you pay for the house to more than cover any fee you agreed to pay.

Q. Why should I use a REALTOR or Realtist?

A. Real estate licensees who are entitled to use the terms REALTOR or Realtist have agreed to follow a code of ethics. These professionals take extra training courses and are involved in the community. Every effort is made to expel members who fail to meet professional standards in serving the public. Many REALTORS seek to improve their professionalism by taking courses and passing difficult tests for additional professional designations.

Q. Who does my real estate agent represent?

A. Unless you have an agreement that your agent represents you (a buyer's agent), in most states your agent isn't actually your agent. By law, she must represent the seller. This means all confidential information you share must be disclosed to the seller and is thus not truly confidential.

Q. What is a dual agent?

A. A dual agent has the permission from both you and the seller to represent both of you in the same transaction. This means that the agent doesn't truly represent either side and is thus more facilitator than agent.

Q. What is an "exclusive" listing?

A. An "exclusive listing" is an agreement between the seller and a real estate broker that specifies under which circumstances the broker has earned a commission. These circumstances depend on what type of listing the "exclusive" is. It's either an "exclusive agency" listing or an "exclusive right to sell" listing. If it is an exclusive agency listing, the seller does not owe a commission if the seller himself sells the house without the assistance of the broker. With an exclusive right to sell listing, the broker is absolutely entitled to a commission if the house sells during the listing period.

> Real estate licensees who are entitled to use the terms REALTOR or Realtist have agreed to follow a code of ethics.

Q. What is MLS?

A. MLS means "multiple listing service." This is when brokers in a community agree to "pool" their listing so that any broker can sell a house and share a commission, no matter with whom the house was originally listed.

 # SEARCHING FOR A HOME

Q. What is an "open house"?

A. This is a marketing tool. A house that's for sale is made available to anyone who wants to go in and see it. In many real estate markets, open houses are available on Sundays and Wednesdays. The agent at the open house always represents the seller.

Q. How can I find out if a house is in a flood plain?

A. Ask your sales agent or check on the Internet. Also check with your insurance agent. You can't always tell by looking around. Ninety percent of homes in the U.S. are subject to some flooding risk. To obtain FEMA (Federal Emergency Management Agency) flood maps, contact:

Map Service Center
P.O. Box 1038
Jessup, Maryland 20794-1038
Phone: (800) 358-9616
Fax: (800) 358-9620

Q. How can I tell if my community contains dangerous environmental conditions?

A. HUD makes environmental maps available on its Web site. Go to http://www.hud.gov/community and click on maps (E-maps). You will be taken to a map of the United States. Click on your state. Click on the area of the state in which you live. If you want more detail, keep clicking. You will find a great deal of environmental information on the map.

Q. Is "gentrification" a good thing?

A. Yes. It means that people are starting to rehabilitate a blighted neighborhood. As this process continues, prices are expected to increase.

Q. Should I buy a "fixer-upper"?

A. How solid is your marriage? Fixer-uppers can take a lot of time and money to renovate. This can place strain on any family's relationships. Often, you don't save as much money as you thought you would. However, if you know what you are doing, are handy with tools, and aren't afraid of hard work, a fixer-upper may be for you. If a fixer-upper is priced correctly, your "sweat-equity" can result in a very nice home at a bargain price.

Q. Is a Home Warranty a Good Buy?

A. A home warranty is no substitute for a thorough inspection. It is a good buy only if the builder or company backing it has a good reputation for timely warranty repairs.

Q. What is a Seller Disclosure or Property Condition Disclosure?

A. This is a signed statement or checklist provided by a seller in which the seller discloses all known defects in the property. In many states, this disclosure is mandatory. The disclosure is an extremely informative document and should be examined carefully prior to inspecting a house.

> If you know what you are doing, are handy with tools, and aren't afraid of hard work, a fixer-upper may be for you.

Q. What do I do if a broker refuses to show me certain neighborhoods?

A. The broker may be guilty of "steering," which is a violation of the Federal Fair Housing Law. Call your state's civil rights commission or the U.S. Department of Housing and Urban Development.

Q. What is a CMA?

A. A CMA is a comparative market study prepared by a broker. It shows recent sales of comparable properties and a likely price range for the subject property. Although this is usually not as accurate as an appraisal, the CMA allows you to make a judgment about how much you should offer for the house.

Q. How many homes should I look at before making an offer?

A. From fifteen to thirty are recommended. So you don't suffer from information overload, take photos and make notes.

The broker normally doesn't want you to see more than five to ten houses. For most brokers, time is money. By limiting the buyer's choices, it's more likely that the buyer will quickly choose a satisfactory house. This benefits the broker but does not always allow you to find the best choice available in the market. Take the time necessary so you feel comfortable that you understand the market. You're the one who's going to make mortgage payments for thirty years. An extra day or two of looking is time well spent.

REAL ESTATE CONTRACTS

Q. **I want to submit an offer to the seller, but the broker says it is too low, and she won't present it. Is there anything I can do?**

A. By law, the broker must present the contract. Advise the broker you will call the state real estate commission. This is usually very effective in motivating the broker to obey the law.

Q. **What is meant by "as is"?**

A. This is a phrase in a contract that means that the seller is making no promises about the condition of the home. You are agreeing to buy the house with all its defects. You are also giving up your right to sue if the house has serious problems that you haven't been told about.

Q. **What is "time is of the essence"?**

A. This phrase means that all time deadlines will be strictly kept.

Q. **What is "equitable conversion"?**

A. This doctrine applies in some states and not in others. If you sign a contract that has no unresolved contingencies, you have the risk of loss even if closing has not yet occurred. In other words, if the house burns down before settlement, you still have to pay for it. The safest thing to do is have a statement in the contract that states that risk of loss does not shift until you have accepted the deed or taken possession of the house.

Q. **What is "earnest money"?**

A. This is money you pay when you sign the contract. Normally, if you fail to perform the contract, you could lose all the earnest money you deposited.

Q. **What is the difference between a "contingency" and a "condition"?**

A. These words mean the same thing. Some people say "contingency," and other people say "condition." In contracts, these are provisions that specify that a certain event must occur before you are obligated to perform on a contract (for example, this contract is contingent on your being approved for a loan). These can also be provisions that free you of an obligation (for example, this contract is conditioned by a satisfactory report from a building inspector).

 # MORTGAGES AND FINANCE

Q. **What is APR?**

A. This is the annual percentage rate disclosure required by the Truth-in-Lending law.

Q. **How can you find out about your credit rating?**

A. Three major companies keep your credit history. You can contact any of these to buy a copy of your credit report. There are numerous Web sites that can help you get this information as well.

Equifax
http://equifax.com
(800) 685-1111
E-mail: customer.care@equifax.com
Equifax Credit Information Services, Inc.
P.O. Box 740241
Atlanta, GA 30374

Experian (formerly TRW)
http://www.experian.com
(800) 397-3742
(800) 972-0322 (for deaf or hearing-impaired)
National Consumer Assistance Center
P.O. Box 2002
Allen, TX 75013
See Web site for local addresses in the U.S.A.

TransUnion
http://www.tuc.com
(800) 888-4213
TransUnion
P.O. Box 2000
Chester, PA 19022

Q. **What is the difference between pre-qualifying and pre-approval for a loan?**

A. Pre-qualifying is an estimate by the lender of the maximum amount of loan you could receive based on your current income and savings if you have good credit. The lender does not give you any kind of commitment. Pre-approval is a commitment by the lender to lend you a certain loan if the house you buy appraises properly and does not have any other deficiencies.

Q. **Why do I have to sign a promissory note if I have already signed a mortgage or deed of trust?**

A. A promissory note is a promise to pay back the money you borrow. The mortgage is a pledge of property backing up the promissory note. If you fail to make your payments, you are said to be in default on your mortgage and your house can be foreclosed. Foreclosure means the house will be sold in a public sale, you will be evicted, and your credit rating damaged for many years. You are still personally responsible for paying

> If you fail to make your payments, you are said to be in default on your mortgage and your house can be foreclosed.

the loan if the lender receives insufficient money from the sale of the property. The lender can sue for a deficiency judgment based on the promissory note you signed.

Q. **What's the difference between a first (or senior) mortgage and a second (or junior) mortgage?**

A. It's important to know the difference between first mortgages (senior liens) and second mortgages (junior liens). The first mortgage is the mortgage that was first recorded. This mortgage has superior claim on the property to all subsequent mortgages recorded. The only claims superior to the first mortgage are government claims such as tax liens and special claims such as mechanic's liens. A mortgage that is filed later than the first mortgage is called a second or third mortgage. So why is this important? It's simple, if the first mortgage is foreclosed, all junior liens are wiped out and the owners of those liens have no more claim against the property. On the other hand, if the second mortgage is foreclosed, whoever buys the property at the foreclosure sale takes "subject to" the first mortgage and will need to take over the monthly payments. Because the second mortgage is more risky than the first, because it can be wiped out, the interest rates on second mortgages are significantly higher than on firsts. For example, the interest rate on a first mortgage might be 7.5%, while the interest rate on the second might be 11%.

Q. **What's the difference between a "discount point" and a "point for a loan origination fee"?**

A. A point is 1% of the loan. If the loan is for $80,000, one point equals $800. A discount point is prepaid interest. It is used to reduce the annual interest you are paying. A point for a loan origination fee is paid to the mortgage broker for finding the money you are borrowing.

Q. **Why do I need mortgage insurance?**

A. If you make less than a 20% down payment, the lender will normally require you to pay for mortgage insurance. This protects the lender if you default on the loan.

Q. **What's the difference between PMI and MIP?**

A. PMI stands for Private Mortgage Insurance, or Premium Mortgage Insurance. This term is used with insurance on conventional loans. MIP stands for Mortgage Insurance Premium charged by FHA. The mortgage insurance is referred to as Mutual Mortgage Insurance (MMI). Beginning January 1, 2001, the upfront mortgage insurance premium charged by FHA is 1.5% of the loan amount. The monthly mortgage insurance payment will be cancelled automatically when the outstanding principal balance reaches 78% of the original purchase price.

Q. **Do lenders offer special mortgage loan programs for first-time buyers?**

A. Yes. Ask your lender, mortgage banker, or local state finance agency if any programs are available in your area.

Q. What does PITI mean?

A. PITI stands for "principal, interest, taxes, and insurance."

Q. What's an impound account, and why do I have to have one?

A. Unless you have made a substantial down payment, lenders require that some money be set aside each month for making future payments. This is an account used by the lender to make sure you pay your fire and hazard insurance and mortgage insurance costs. Each month a portion of your monthly mortgage payment includes an amount that is collected for this impound account.

Q. Is a fixed-rate mortgage better than an adjustable-rate mortgage (ARM)?

A. It depends on how high the interest rates are and how long you plan to stay. If interest rates are low, seriously consider a fixed-rate mortgage. If rates are high and you expect them to be lower in the future, an ARM is a good idea. If you expect to move in the next few years, an ARM is worth considering.

> If interest rates are low, seriously consider a fixed-rate mortgage. If rates are high and you expect them to be lower in the future, an ARM is a good idea.

Q. What is a "teaser rate"?

A. A teaser rate is a very low initial mortgage rate for an ARM mortgage. It's used to entice new borrowers. After a short time, the rate is adjusted to a much higher normal rate.

Q. What is FHA?

A. FHA is the Federal Housing Administration, an agency within the Department of Housing and Urban Development. It provides lenders with mortgage insurance, making it possible for borrowers with special needs to qualify for mortgage loans. FHA-insured loans carry much more liberal qualifying ratios than do conventional loans.

Q. What is a "due on sale" clause?

A. This clause requires a borrower to pay off the mortgage balance if a house is sold or leased for a long term. This prevents new borrowers from assuming a mortgage without first getting approval and usually paying new fees to the lender.

Q. What is a pre-payment penalty clause?

A. Many mortgages do not allow pre-payments or partial pre-payments of a mortgage without the payment of a penalty. In some cases, the penalty can be substantial. Usually, these penalties exist for the first five years of the loan, but they can last longer.

 # TITLE INSURANCE AND CLOSING

Q. What is a "chain of title?

A. This is the history of owners and lien holders who held interests in a particular property.

Q. What is an "abstract of title"?

A. This is a summary of all documents in the chain of title. An attorney or professional abstractor prepares it.

Q. What is a "cloud on title"?

A. This is a title defect that prevents title from being marketable.

Q. What is an "owner's policy"?

A. Title insurance consists of a lender's or mortgagee's policy and an owner's policy. The lender's policy protects the lender for up to the amount of the remaining mortgage balance. It provides no protection for the borrower even though the borrower has paid the one-time premium for this insurance. To obtain protection for the owner's equity interest in the property, it's necessary to purchase additional insurance through an owner's policy.

Q. What is escrow?

A. Escrow involves closing a transaction through the facilities of an objective third party who is given written instructions by the buyer and seller. Many states use escrow to close a transaction; other states use a settlement attorney who closes a transaction with all parties present.

Q. What is RESPA?

A. RESPA is a federal law called the Real Estate Settlement Procedures Act. It establishes a number of disclosure requirements on the lender throughout the loan process. These disclosures include costs associated with the closing and revelation of business relationships among various companies providing services in the transaction.

Q. What is a "Good Faith Estimate"?

A. This must be provided to the borrower within three days of a loan application. It contains estimates of closing costs and is required by RESPA.

Q. Why should I insist on a final walk-through?

A. After a deed is delivered and accepted, the contract is merged into the deed. If the seller has failed to make agreed repairs or has removed property like an expensive light fixture or a refrigerator you thought you had bought, you may discover you have lost your rights to these. It's essential that you do a final walk-through, preferably the day of the closing, to solve problems or set money aside in escrow before the actual settlement.

A FINAL QUESTION

Q. **What's it like to own my own home?**

A. Initially, it's like living in a dream. Enjoy it before reality sets in and you have to mow the lawn or shovel snow from the sidewalk. The biggest payoff is when you sell it and find out how much more equity you have compared to friends who were renting and therefore have nothing to show for their housing payments except rental receipts.

Index